# YOUR RIGHTS UNDER THE FAMILY AND MEDICAL LEAVE ACT

*by*
Margaret C. Jasper

Oceana's Legal Almanac Series:
*Law for the Layperson*

2005
Oceana Publications
A Division of Oxford University Press, Inc.

Information contained in this work has been obtained by Oceana Publications from sources believed to be reliable. However, neither the Publisher nor its authors guarantee the accuracy or completeness of any information published herein, and neither the Publisher nor its authors shall be responsible for any errors, omissions or damages arising from the use of this information. This work is published with the understanding that the Publisher and its authors are supplying information, but are not attempting to render legal or other professional services. If such services are required, the assistance of an appropriate professional should be sought.

You may order this or any Oceana publication by visiting Oceana's website at http://www.oceanalaw.com

Library of Congress Control Number: 2005934461

ISBN 0-379-11398-8

Oceana's Legal Almanac Series: Law for the Layperson
ISSN 1075-7376

©2005 Oceana Publications, a division of Oxford University Press, Inc.

Manufactured in the United States of America on acid-free paper.

To My Husband Chris

Your love and support
are my motivation and inspiration

-and-

In memory of my son, Jimmy

# Table of Contents

## CHAPTER 6:
## MEDICAL CERTIFICATION REQUIREMENT

## CHAPTER 7:
## JOB PROTECTION

## CHAPTER 8:
## EMPLOYER RESPONSIBILITIES

# ABOUT THE AUTHOR

MARGARET C. JASPER is an attorney engaged in the general practice of law in South Salem, New York, concentrating in the areas of personal injury and entertainment law. Ms. Jasper holds a Juris Doctor degree from Pace University School of Law, White Plains, New York, is a member of the New York and Connecticut bars, and is certified to practice before the United States District Courts for the Southern and Eastern Districts of New York, the United States Court of Appeals for the Second Circuit, and the United States Supreme Court.

Ms. Jasper has been appointed to the panel of arbitrators of the American Arbitration Association and the law guardian panel for the Family Court of the State of New York, is a member of the Association of Trial Lawyers of America, and is a New York State licensed real estate broker and member of the Westchester County Board of Realtors, operating as Jasper Real Estate, in South Salem, New York. Margaret Jasper maintains a website at http://www.JasperLawOffice.com.

Ms. Jasper is the author and general editor of the following legal almanacs: AIDS Law; The Americans with Disabilities Act; Animal Rights Law; The Law of Attachment and Garnishment; Bankruptcy Law for the Individual Debtor; Individual Bankruptcy and Restructuring; Banks and their Customers; Becoming a Citizen; Buying and Selling Your Home; The Law of Buying and Selling; The Law of Capital Punishment; The Law of Child Custody; Your Rights in a Class Action Suit; Commercial Law; Consumer Rights Law; The Law of Contracts; Co-ops and Condominiums: Your Rights and Obligations As Owner; Copyright Law; Credit Cards and the Law; The Law of Debt Collection; Dictionary of Selected Legal Terms; The Law of Dispute Resolution; Drunk Driving Law; DWI, DUI and the Law; Education Law; Elder Law; Employee Rights in the Workplace; Employment Discrimination Under Title VII; Environmental Law; Estate Planning; Everyday Legal Forms; Executors and Personal Representatives: Rights and Responsibilities; Harassment in the Workplace; Health Care and Your Rights; Hiring Household Help and Contractors: Your Rights and Obligations Under the Law; Home Mortgage Law Primer; Hospital Liability Law; How To Change Your Name; How To Protect Your Challenged Child; Identity Theft and How To Protect Yourself; Insurance Law; The Law of Immigration; International Adoption; Juvenile Justice and Children's Law; Labor Law; Landlord-Tenant Law; The Law of Libel and Slander; Living Together: Practical Legal Issues; Marriage and Divorce; The Law of Medical Malpractice; Motor Vehicle Law; The Law of No-Fault Insurance; Nursing Home Negligence; The Law of Obscenity and Pornography; Patent Law; The Law of Personal Injury; The Law of Premises Liability; Prescription Drugs; Privacy and the Internet: Your Rights and Expectations Under the Law; Probate Law; The Law of Product Liability; Real Estate Law for the Homeowner and Broker; Religion and the Law; Retirement Planning; The Right to Die; Rights of Single Parents; Law for the Small Business Owner; Small Claims Court; Social Security Law; Special Education Law; The Law of Speech and the First Amendment; Teenagers and Substance Abuse; Trademark Law; Victim's Rights Law; The Law of Violence Against Women; Welfare: Your Rights and the Law; What if it Happened to You: Violent Crimes and Victims' Rights; What if the Product Doesn't Work: Warranties & Guarantees; Workers' Compensation Law; and Your Child's Legal Rights: An Overview.

# INTRODUCTION

The most vulnerable of America's population—the children and the elderly—are becoming increasingly dependent upon family members who are forced to spend long hours at work in order to make ends meet. When a family emergency arises, an employee is faced with deciding whether they should stay home to attend to a sick child or elderly parent and risk the possibility of losing their job and benefits.

It was recognized that America's workers need reassurance that they will not be asked to choose between continuing their employment, and attending to serious personal and family obligations. In 1993, the Family and Medical Leave Act (FMLA) was enacted to help employees faced with these difficult choices. The FMLA allows an employee to balance their work and family responsibilities by taking reasonable unpaid leave for certain family and medical reasons.

This almanac analyzes the FMLA and its various provisions, including the circumstances under which unpaid leave may be granted; eligibility; notification requirements; medical certification; employment and job benefits protection; employer responsibilities, and enforcement measures.

The Appendix provides applicable statutes, sample forms, and other pertinent information and data. The Glossary contains definitions of many of the terms used throughout the almanac.

# CHAPTER 1:
# WHAT IS THE FAMILY AND MEDICAL LEAVE ACT?

## PURPOSE OF THE FAMILY AND MEDICAL LEAVE ACT OF 1993

In an increasing number of American families, both parents work outside the home. In addition, there are many families headed by a single working parent. Many families are taking care of young children and elderly parents, and working parents are faced with the possibility of losing their job if they take time from work to attend to a sick family member, to attend to their own health needs, or to care for a newborn or newly adopted baby.

On February 5, 1993, The Family and Medical Leave Act (FMLA) was enacted. The FMLA became effective for most employers on August 5, 1993. The FMLA was intended to help employees balance their work and family responsibilities by allowing them to take a reasonable amount of unpaid leave for certain family and medical reasons. It was recognized that this would promote both the stability and economic security of families, as well as the national interest in preserving family integrity. In addition, the FMLA was expected to benefit employers. In fact, statistics show that employees who have a stable family life are more productive in the workplace. The FMLA was also designed to minimize the potential for employment discrimination on the basis of sex, while promoting equal employment opportunity for men and women.

The text of the Family and Medical Leave Act is set forth at Appendix 1.

## BASIC PROVISIONS OF THE FMLA

Following are the basic provisions of the FMLA, which are discussed in more depth elsewhere in this almanac.

### Unpaid Job-Protected Leave

The most important provision of the FMLA is the employee's right to unpaid job-protected leave under certain circumstances. The FMLA provides that a "covered employer" must grant an "eligible employee" up to 12 weeks of unpaid, job-protected leave per year. If the employee has earned or accrued paid leave, such leave may be substituted instead of unpaid leave. If the employee does not elect to substitute paid leave, the employer may require the use of accrued paid leave. In certain cases, FMLA leave may be taken on an intermittent basis—i.e., in segments—rather than all at once, or the employee may work a part-time schedule, known as a reduced leave schedule.

Under the FMLA, the circumstances which trigger the employee's right to take FMLA leave include: (1) the birth of an employee's son or daughter and care of the newborn; (2) placement of a child with the employee for adoption or foster care; (3) the employee's own serious health condition which makes the employee unable to perform the functions of his or her job; or (4) the need to care for an immediate family member—i.e., a child, spouse, or parent—with a serious health condition.

The reasons an employee may request FMLA leave are discussed more fully in Chapter 4 of this almanac.

### Maintenance of Group Health Benefits

Another important provision of the FMLA is the employee's right to have their health benefits maintained while on FMLA leave as if the employee had continued to work instead of taking the leave. In addition, the employer must continue to pay whatever share of the employee's health care premium the employer was paying prior to the employee's leave period. If an employee was paying all or part of the premium payments prior to taking leave, the employee must continue to pay his or her share during their leave period. The employer may recover its share only if the employee does not return to work for a reason other than the serious health condition of the employee or the employee's immediate family member, or another reason beyond the employee's control.

### Job Protection

Under the FMLA, an employee generally has the right to return to the same position or an equivalent position with equivalent pay, benefits and working conditions at the conclusion of the leave. In fact, taking FMLA leave cannot result in the loss of any employee benefit that accrued prior to the start of the leave.

The employer has the right to 30 days' advance notice from the employee that he or she will be taking FMLA leave, if practicable. In addition, the employer may require an employee to submit certification from a health care provider to substantiate that the leave is due to the serious health condition of the employee or the employee's immediate family member. Failure to comply with these requirements may result in a delay in the start of FMLA leave.

The employer may also require that an employee present a certification of fitness to return to work when the absence was caused by the employee's own serious health condition. The employer may delay restoring the employee to employment if the employee does not present such a certificate relating to the health condition that caused their absence.

The responsibilities of both the employer and employee, including medical certification, are discussed more fully elsewhere in this almanac.

## WHO IS CONSIDERED A HEALTH CARE PROVIDER UNDER THE FMLA?

For purposes of the FMLA, the term "health care provider" includes:

1. A doctor of medicine or osteopathy who is authorized to practice medicine or surgery by the State in which the doctor practices; or

2. Any other person determined by the Secretary to be capable of providing health care services, including:

(a) Podiatrists, dentists, clinical psychologists, optometrists, and chiropractors authorized to practice in the State and performing within the scope of their practice as defined under State law;

(b) Nurse practitioners, nurse-midwives and clinical social workers who are authorized to practice under State law and who are performing within the scope of their practice as defined under State law;

(c) Christian Science practitioners listed with the First Church of Christ, Scientist in Boston, Massachusetts. However, if an employee or family member is being treated by a Christian Science practitioner, the employee may not object to any requirement from an employer that the employee or family member submit to an examination in order to obtain a second or third certification from a health care provider other than a Christian Science practitioner.

(d) Any health care provider from whom an employer or the employer's group health plan's benefits manager will accept certification of the existence of a serious health condition to substantiate a claim for benefits; and

(e) A health care provider listed above who practices in a country other than the United States, who is authorized to practice in accordance with the law of that country, and who is performing within the scope of his or her practice as defined under such law.

## WAIVER OF FMLA RIGHTS

Employees cannot waive—nor may employers induce employees to waive—their rights under the FMLA. For example, employees, or their collective bargaining representatives, cannot "trade off" the right to take FMLA leave against some other benefit offered by the employer.

# CHAPTER 2:
# WHAT IS A COVERED EMPLOYER?

## IN GENERAL

The FMLA sets forth specific rules which govern whether an employer is covered by the FMLA. The rules vary according to whether the employer is a private company or a public agency or school, as further discussed below. It should be noted, however, that regardless of whether the employer is a covered employer under the FMLA, the employee must meet all of the eligibility requirements set forth in the FMLA in order to qualify for FMLA leave.

Employee eligibility requirements are discussed more fully in Chapter 3 of this almanac.

## PRIVATE COMPANIES

### The 50 Employees/20 Workweeks Threshold

Under the FMLA, an employer engaged in commerce, or in any industry or activity affecting commerce, who employs 50 or more employees for each working day during each of 20 or more calendar workweeks in the current or preceding calendar year, is considered a covered employer under the FMLA. It is not necessary for the workweeks to run consecutively to be counted. For purposes of the FMLA, employers who meet the 50-employee coverage test are deemed to be engaged in commerce or in an industry or activity affecting commerce.

Once the employer meets the 50 employees/20 workweeks threshold, the employer remains a covered employer until it reaches a future point where it no longer employs 50 employees for 20 nonconsecutive workweeks in the current or preceding calendar year.

For example, if an employer who met the 50 employees/20 workweeks test in the calendar year as of August 5, 2005, subsequently dropped below 50 employees before the end of 2005, and continued to employ fewer than 50 employees in all workweeks throughout calendar year 2006, the employer would continue to be considered a covered employer for purposes of the FMLA throughout calendar year 2006, because the employer met the coverage criteria of "50 employees/20 workweeks in the preceding (2005) calendar year." However, if the employer continued to employ fewer than 50 employees throughout calendar year 2007, the employer would not be considered a covered employer in calendar year 2007 because the employer no longer met the "50 employees/20 workweeks in the current (2007) or preceding (2006) calendar year" threshold.

### Counting Employees for Purposes of FMLA Coverage

The FMLA only applies to employees who are employed within any State of the United States, the District of Columbia or any territory or possession of the United States. Employees who are employed outside these areas are not counted for purposes of determining employer coverage or employee eligibility.

Any employee whose name appears on the employer's payroll will be considered employed each working day of the calendar week, and must be counted, whether or not the employee receives any compensation for that week. This includes part-time employees. However, if an employee does not begin to work for the employer until after the first working day of a calendar week, that employee is not considered employed on each working day of that calendar week and would not be counted.

Employees on paid or unpaid leave, including FMLA leave, leaves of absence, disciplinary suspension, etc., are counted as long as the employer has a reasonable expectation that the employee will later return to active employment. However, where there is no longer an employer/employee relationship—e.g. when an employee is laid off—that employee does not have to be counted. In addition, an employee who is terminated before the last working day of a calendar week, is not considered employed on each working day of that calendar week, and is not counted.

### Persons Acting in Interest of Covered Employer

In addition to the covered employer, any person acting, directly or indirectly, in the interest of a covered employer, to a covered employee, is subject to the provisions of the FMLA. For example, individuals such as corporate officers who act in the interest of an employer are individually liable for any violations of FMLA requirements.

### Successor In Interest

Any successor in interest of a covered employer is also subject to the provisions of the FMLA. A determination of whether or not a successor in interest relationship exists is not determined by the application of any single criterion, but rather the entire circumstances are to be viewed in their totality. In order to determine whether an entity is a successor in interest of a covered employer for purposes of the FMLA, the following factors are considered:

1. Substantial continuity of the same business operations;
2. Use of the same plant;
3. Continuity of the work force;
4. Similarity of jobs and working conditions;
5. Similarity of supervisory personnel;
6. Similarity in machinery, equipment, and production methods;
7. Similarity of products or services; and
8. The ability of the predecessor to provide relief.

When an employer is deemed a successor in interest, the employees' entitlements are the same as if the employment by the predecessor and successor were continuous employment by a single employer. For example, the successor, whether or not it meets FMLA coverage criteria, must grant leave for eligible employees who had provided appropriate notice to the predecessor, and must continue leave begun by eligible employees while employed by the predecessor. The successor must also maintain all benefits for those employees taking FMLA leave, including group health benefits during the employees' leave, and job restoration at the conclusion of their leave period.

In addition, a successor which meets the FMLA's coverage criteria must also count periods of employment and hours worked for the predecessor for purposes of determining employee eligibility for FMLA leave.

### The Integrated Employer

Generally, the legal entity which employs the employee is considered the covered employer under the FMLA. Thus, a corporation is a single employer. However, where one corporation has an ownership interest in another corporation, each is considered a separate employer for purposes of the FMLA unless the corporations are deemed "integrated employers." If so, the separate entities will be deemed parts of a single employer, and the employees of all of the entities will be counted to determine employer coverage and employee eligibility.

In order to determine whether two or more separate entities are an integrated employer for purposes of the FMLA, the following factors will be considered:

1. Common management;

2. Interrelation between operations;

3. Centralized control of labor relations; and

4. Degree of common ownership and financial control.

### Joint Employers

If two or more businesses exercise some control over the work or working conditions of the employee, the businesses may be considered joint employers under the FMLA. Joint employers may be separate and distinct entities with separate owners, managers and facilities. Where the employee performs work that simultaneously benefits two or more employers, or works for two or more employers at different times during the workweek, a joint employment relationship generally will be considered to exist.

A determination of whether or not a joint employment relationship exists is not determined by the application of any single criterion, but rather the entire relationship is to be viewed in its totality. Factors to be considered include:

1. Whether there is an arrangement between employers to share an employee's services or to interchange employees;

2. Whether one employer acts directly or indirectly in the interest of the other employer in relation to the employee; or,

3. Whether the employers are not completely disassociated with respect to the employee's employment, and may be deemed to share control of the employee, directly or indirectly, because one employer controls, is controlled by, or is under common control with the other employer.

For example, joint employment will ordinarily be found to exist when a temporary or leasing agency supplies employees to a second employer.

In joint employment relationships, only the primary employer is responsible for giving required notices to its employees, providing FMLA leave, and maintenance of health benefits. Factors to be considered in determining which entity is the "primary'" employer for purposes of the FMLA include:

1. Which employer has the authority to hire and fire the employee;

2. Which employer is responsible for assigning and/or placing the employee;

3. Which employer is responsible for making the payroll; and

4. Which employer is responsible for providing employment benefits.

For example, for employees of temporary help or leasing agencies, the placement agency most commonly would be considered the primary employer.

Employees jointly employed by two employers must be counted by both employers, whether or not maintained on one of the employer's payroll, in determining employer coverage and employee eligibility under the FMLA. For example, an employer who jointly employs 15 workers from a leasing or temporary help agency and also employs 40 permanent workers is covered by the FMLA. In addition, an employee on leave who is working for a secondary employer is considered employed by the secondary employer, and must be counted for coverage and eligibility purposes, as long as the employer has a reasonable expectation that the employee will return to employment with that employer.

## PUBLIC AGENCIES

Public agencies are covered employers under the FMLA regardless of the number of employees employed by the agency. Public agencies for purposes of the FMLA include:

1. The government of the United States;

2. The government of a State or political subdivision of a State;

3. An agency of the United States, a State, or a political subdivision of a State; or

4. Any interstate governmental agency.

The term "State" includes any State of the United States, the District of Columbia, or any Territory or possession of the United States.

### Employees of Public Agencies

For purposes of determining employee eligibility under the FMLA, a public agency is considered a single employer, e.g., a State is a single employer; a county is a single employer; and a city or town is a single employer

## SCHOOLS

Public schools and private elementary and secondary schools are covered employers under the FMLA regardless of the number of employees employed by the school. Nevertheless, all of the employee eligibility requirements do apply, as discussed in Chapter 3. This includes the requirement that an employee must be employed at a worksite where at least 50 employees are employed within 75 miles.

For example, employees of a rural school would not be eligible for FMLA leave if the school has fewer than 50 employees and there are no other schools under the jurisdiction of the same employer—e.g., the school board—within 75 miles.

# CHAPTER 3:
# WHAT IS AN ELIGIBLE EMPLOYEE?

## ELIGIBILITY

An employee is considered eligible for FMLA leave provided they meet the following requirements:

1. The employee employed by a covered employer, as set forth in Chapter 2 of this almanac; and

2. The employee has been employed by the employer for at least 12 months; and

3. The employee has been employed for at least 1,250 hours of service during the 12-month period immediately preceding the commencement of the leave; and

4. The employee is employed at a worksite where 50 or more employees are employed by the employer within 75 miles of that worksite.

## THE 12-MONTH REQUIREMENT

The 12 months an employee must have been employed by the employer need not run consecutively. If an employee is maintained on the payroll for any part of a week, the week counts as a week of employment. This would include any periods of paid or unpaid leave, sick time, or vacation time, during which other benefits or compensation are provided by the employer—e.g., workers' compensation, group health plan benefits, etc.

## THE 1,250 HOURS OF SERVICE REQUIREMENT

In order to determine whether the employee has worked the minimum 1,250 hours of service to be eligible for FMLA coverage, any accurate accounting of actual hours worked may be used. In the event an employer does not maintain an accurate record of hours worked by an employee, the employer has the burden of showing that the employee has not worked the required number of hours. In the event the employer is unable to meet this burden of proof, the employee is deemed to have met this test. An employer must be able to clearly demonstrate that the employee did not work 1,250 hours during the previous 12 months in order to claim that the employee is not eligible for FMLA leave.

It should be noted that a full-time teacher in an elementary or secondary school system, or institution of higher education, or other educational establishment or institution is deemed to have satisfied the 1,250 hour test.

### THE 50 EMPLOYEES WITHIN 75 MILES OF WORKSITE DETERMINATION

For purposes of employee eligibility, in determining whether the employer employs 50 employees within 75 miles of the employee's worksite, a worksite can refer to either a single location or a group of contiguous locations. For example, buildings that form a campus or industrial park may be considered a single site of employment.

In addition, separate buildings or areas which are not directly connected or in immediate proximity are considered a single worksite if they are in reasonable geographic proximity to each other, are used for the same purpose, and share the same staff and equipment. For example, if an employer manages a number of warehouses in a metropolitan area, but regularly shifts or rotates the same employees from one building to another, the multiple warehouses would be considered a single worksite.

Alternatively, there may be several single sites of employment within a single building, such as an office building, if separate employers conduct activities within the building. For example, an office building with 50 different businesses as tenants will contain 50 sites of employment. The offices of each employer will be considered separate sites of employment for purposes of the FMLA.

An employee's worksite under the FMLA will ordinarily be the site the employee reports to, or the location where the employee receives his or her work assignment. For example, for employees who have no fixed worksite, e.g., construction workers, transportation workers, salespersons, etc., the worksite may be: (1) the site to which they are assigned as their home base; (2) the site from which their work is assigned; or (3) the site to which they report.

For purposes of determining an employee's eligibility when the employee is jointly employed by two or more employers, the employee's worksite is the primary employer's office from which the employee is assigned or reports. The employee is also counted by the secondary employer to determine eligibility for the secondary employer's full-time or permanent employees.

The 75-mile distance is measured by surface miles, using surface transportation over public streets, roads, highways and waterways, by the shortest route from the facility where the eligible employee requesting leave is employed. If there is no available surface transportation between the worksites, the distance is measured by using the most frequently utilized mode of transportation.

The determination of how many employees are employed within 75 miles of the worksite of the employee requesting FMLA leave is based on the number of employees maintained on the payroll. It should be noted that employees of educational institutions who are employed permanently, or who are under contract are considered maintained on the payroll during any portion of the year when school is not in session.

## TIMING OF ELIGIBILITY DETERMINATION

The determination of whether an employee has worked for the employer for at least 1,250 hours in the past 12 months and has been employed by the employer for a total of at least 12 months must be made as of the date leave commences. If an employee notifies the employer of the need for FMLA leave before the employee meets the eligibility criteria, the employer must either confirm the employee's eligibility based upon a projection that the employee will be eligible on the date leave would commence, or must advise the employee when the eligibility requirement will be satisfied.

If the employer confirms eligibility at the time the notice for leave is received, the employer may not subsequently challenge the employee's eligibility. In the latter case, if the employer does not advise the employee whether the employee is eligible as soon as practicable—i.e., two business days absent extenuating circumstances—after the date employee eligibility is determined, the employee will have satisfied the notice requirements and the notice of leave is considered current and outstanding until the employer does advise the employee of his or her eligibility status. If the employer fails to advise the employee whether the employee is eligible prior to the date the requested leave is to commence, the employee will be deemed eligible. In that case, the employer may not deny the employee's FMLA leave request.

The Department of Labor has developed an optional form (DOL Form WH-381) for employers to use to notify an employee as to their eligibility status.

A copy of an Employer Response to Employee Request for Family or Medical Leave [DOL Form WH-381] is set forth at Appendix 2.

If the employee does not give the employer notice of the need for leave more than two business days prior to commencing leave, the employee will be deemed eligible if the employer fails to advise the employee that the employee is not eligible within two business days of receiving the employee's notice.

The eligibility requirement that 50 employees are employed within 75 miles of the employee's worksite is determined when the employee gives notice of the need for leave. Once an employee is determined eligible, the employee's eligibility is not affected by any subsequent change in the number of employees employed at or within 75 miles of the employee's worksite.

Similarly, an employer may not terminate employee leave that has already started if the employee count drops below 50 within 75 miles of the employee's worksite. For example, if an employer employs 60 employees in August, but expects that the number of employees will drop to 40 in December, the employer must grant FMLA benefits to an otherwise eligible employee who gives notice of the need for leave in August for a period of leave to begin in December.

### EMPLOYEES OF PUBLIC AGENCIES

For purposes of determining employee eligibility under the FMLA, a public agency is considered a single employer, e.g., a State is a single employer; a county is a single employer; and a city or town is a single employer. In addition, employees of public agencies must meet all of the eligibility requirements set forth above.

# CHAPTER 4:
# UNDER WHAT CIRCUMSTANCES IS AN EMPLOYEE ENTITLED TO TAKE FMLA LEAVE?

## COVERED CIRCUMSTANCES

The FMLA sets forth those circumstances which trigger the employee's right to take FMLA leave, including:

1. The birth of a son or daughter, and time to care for the newborn child;

2. Placement with the employee of a son or daughter for adoption or foster care;

3. Leave needed to attend to a serious health condition that makes the employee unable to perform the functions of the employee's job; and

4. Leave needed to care for the employee's spouse, son, daughter, or parent with a serious health condition.

## BIRTH OF A SON OR DAUGHTER

An employee is entitled to take FMLA leave for the birth of their son or daughter, and to take care of the newborn baby. This entitlement to FMLA leave expires at the end of the 12-month period that begins on the date of the baby's birth. However, certain circumstances may require that FMLA leave begin before the actual date of birth of a child. For example, an expectant mother may take FMLA leave before the birth of the child for prenatal care or if she is unable to work due to her condition.

The right to take FMLA leave for the birth and care of a baby applies equally to male and female employees. For example, the father, as well as the mother, can take family leave for the birth and care of their child. However, if a husband and wife are employed by the same covered employer, their FMLA leave may be limited to a combined total of 12 weeks from the date of birth.

### PLACEMENT OF A SON OR DAUGHTER FOR ADOPTION OR FOSTER CARE

An employee is entitled to take FMLA leave for the placement of a son or daughter with the employee for adoption or foster care. This entitlement to FMLA leave expires at the end of the 12-month period that begins on the date of placement. In addition, covered employers are required to grant FMLA leave before the actual placement or adoption of a child if an absence from work is required for the placement to proceed, e.g. to appear in court, attend counseling sessions, etc.

The right to take FMLA leave for the placement of a son or daughter applies equally to male and female employees. For example, the father, as well as the mother, can take family leave for the placement of their child. However, if a husband and wife are employed by the same covered employer, their FMLA leave may be limited to a combined total of 12 weeks from the date of placement.

#### Foster Care

Foster care refers to the care of a child away from, and in substitution for, the child's natural parent or guardian. However, in order to qualify for FMLA leave, state action must be involved in the removal of the child from parental custody. Therefore, if a parent voluntarily places their child with a relative, that relative cannot qualify for FMLA leave.

### SERIOUS HEALTH CONDITION

As set forth above, an employee is entitled to take FMLA leave if the employee suffers from a serious health condition that makes the employee unable to perform the functions of his or her job. An employee may also take FMLA leave if the employee's immediate family member suffers from a serious health condition and the employee is needed to care for the family member.

#### What is Considered a Serious Health Condition?

Under the FMLA, a "serious health condition" is defined as an illness, injury, impairment, or physical or mental condition that involves:

1. Inpatient care in a hospital, hospice, or residential medical care facility, including any period of incapacity, or any subsequent treatment in connection with the employee's inpatient care; or

2. Continuing treatment by a health care provider including any one or more of the following:

(a) A period of incapacity of more than three consecutive calendar days, and any subsequent treatment or period of incapacity relating to the same condition, that also involves:

(i) Treatment two or more times by a health care provider, by a nurse or physician's assistant under direct supervision of a health care provider, or by a provider of health care services under orders of, or on referral by, a health care provider; or

(ii) Treatment by a health care provider on at least one occasion which results in a regimen of continuing treatment under the supervision of the health care provider. Although the FMLA does cover treatments needed to diagnose a serious health condition, it does not cover treatments such as routine physical examinations, eye examinations or dental examinations. A regimen of "continuing treatment" may include, for example, a course of prescription medication or therapy requiring special equipment to resolve or alleviate the health condition. However, a course of continuing treatment that could be initiated without a visit to a health care provider, such as taking over-the-counter medications, drinking fluids, bed rest, and exercise, would not be sufficient to constitute a regimen of continuing treatment for purposes of FMLA leave.

(b) Any period of incapacity due to pregnancy, or for prenatal care. Such absences may qualify for FMLA leave even though the employee or immediate family member does not receive treatment from a health care provider during the absence, and even if the absence does not last more than three days. For example, the employee or immediate family member may be unable to report to work because of severe morning sickness.

(c) Any period of incapacity or treatment for such incapacity due to a chronic serious health condition. A chronic serious health condition is one which:

(i) Requires periodic visits for treatment by a health care provider, or by a nurse or physician's assistant under direct supervision of a health care provider;

(ii) Continues over an extended period of time, including recurring episodes of a single underlying condition; and

(iii) May cause episodic rather than a continuing period of incapacity, e.g., conditions such as asthma, diabetes, epilepsy, etc. As with pregnancy, such absences may qualify for FMLA leave even though the employee or immediate family member does not receive treatment from a health care provider during the absence, and even if the absence does not last more than three days. For example, an employee with asthma may be unable to report for work due to the onset of an asthma attack.

(d) A period of incapacity which is permanent or long-term due to a condition for which treatment may not be effective. The employee or family member must be under the continuing supervision of, but need not be receiving active treatment by, a health care provider. Examples of such conditions include Alzheimer's, a severe stroke, or the terminal stages of a disease.

(e) Any period of absence to receive multiple treatments, including any period of recovery, by a health care provider or by a provider of health care services under orders of, or on referral by, a health care provider, either for restorative surgery after an accident or other injury, or for a condition that would likely result in a period of incapacity of more than three consecutive calendar days in the absence of medical intervention or treatment, e.g., dialysis treatment for kidney disease.

### Substance Abuse Treatment

FMLA leave is available for treatment for substance abuse provided the condition qualifies as a serious health condition, as set forth above. However, FMLA leave may only be taken for treatment for substance abuse by a health care provider or by a provider of health care services on referral by a health care provider.

Nevertheless, treatment for substance abuse does not prevent an employer from taking employment action against an employee. The employer may not take action against the employee because the employee has exercised his or her right to take FMLA leave for treatment. However, if the employer has notified employees of a non-discriminatory, established policy, that provides for the termination of an employee for substance abuse, the employee may be terminated whether or not the employee is presently taking FMLA leave pursuant to that policy. Further, absence because of the employee's use of the substance, rather than for treatment, does not qualify for FMLA leave.

An employee may also take FMLA leave to care for an immediate family member who is receiving treatment for substance abuse. In this situation, the employer may not take action against an employee who is providing care for an immediate family member receiving treatment for substance abuse.

### Inability to Perform Functions of the Position

When an employee requests FMLA leave due to the employee's own serious health condition, the condition must be serious enough to render the employee "unable to perform the functions of the position." In order to qualify, the health care provider must find that the employee is unable to work at all, or is unable to perform any one of the essential functions of the employee's position. In addition, an employee who must be absent from work to receive medical treatment for a serious health condition is also considered "unable to perform the essential functions of the position" during the period the employee is receiving treatment.

An employer has the option, in requiring certification from a health care provider, to provide a statement of the essential functions of the employee's position for the health care provider to review. For purposes of the FMLA, the "essential functions" of the employee's position are those associated with the position the employee held at the time notice is given, or at the time FMLA leave begins, whichever is earlier.

### Conditions Not Covered Under the FMLA

Following are examples of conditions which would not be considered serious health conditions for purposes of the FMLA and, therefore, would not entitle the employee to take FMLA leave:

1. Conditions for which cosmetic treatments are administered, such as plastic surgery, are not considered serious health conditions for purposes of the FMLA unless inpatient hospital care is required, or unless complications develop. However, plastic surgery needed as the result of an injury, for example, would be a covered condition.

2. Common health disorders, such as a cold, the flu, earache, upset stomach, minor ulcers, headaches other than migraine, etc., are not considered serious health conditions for purposes of the FMLA unless complications arise.

3. Routine dental or orthodontia problems, and periodontal disease, etc., are not considered serious health conditions for purposes of the FMLA. However, restorative dental treatment needed as the result of an injury, for example, would be a covered condition.

## IMMEDIATE FAMILY MEMBERS

As set forth above, an employee may take FMLA leave to care for a spouse, son, daughter, or parent suffering from a serious health condition. The employer may require the employee to provide reasonable documentation of the family relationship. Reasonable documentation may include a simple statement from the employee; a child's birth certificate; a court document, etc. The employer is entitled to examine the documents provided, however, the employee is entitled to have those documents returned.

### Spouse

The FMLA defines "spouse" as a husband or wife recognized under State law for purposes of marriage in the State where the employee resides, including common law marriage in the minority of States where such a marriage is still recognized.

### Parent

The FMLA defines "parent" as the biological parent—or an individual who stands or stood in loco parentis—of the employee. Persons who are "in loco parentis" include those with day-to-day responsibilities to care for and financially support a child or, in the case of an employee, the term refers to those persons who had such responsibility for the employee when the employee was a child. A biological or legal relationship is not necessary. For the purposes of the FMLA, "parent" does not include the employee's "parents-in-law."

### Son or Daughter

The FMLA defines a "son" or "daughter" as a biological, adopted, or foster child, a stepchild, a legal ward, or a child of a person standing in loco parentis, who is either under age 18, or age 18 and older, and incapable of self-care because of a mental or physical disability.

### The Employee's Need to Care For a Family Member

An employee is entitled to FMLA leave if he or she is "needed to care for" a family member. This encompasses both physical and psychological care of the family member, and may include the situations described below.

### A Family Member Incapable of Self-Care

A family member may be incapable of self-care due to a serious health condition. "Incapable of self-care" means that the individual requires active assistance or supervision to provide daily self-care in three or more "activities of daily living" (ADLs) or "instrumental activities of daily living" (IADLs). Activities of daily living include adaptive activities such as caring appropriately for one's grooming and hygiene, bathing, dressing and eating. Instrumental activities of daily living include cooking, cleaning, shopping, taking public transportation, paying bills, maintaining a residence, using a telephone, and going to the post office, etc.

### Physical or Mental Disability

A family member may be deemed to have a "physical or mental disability" if he or she suffers from a physical or mental impairment that substantially limits one or more of the major life activities of the individual.

In addition, a family member may be in need of psychological care and comfort while receiving treatment for a serious health condition.

# CHAPTER 5:
# HOW MUCH FMLA LEAVE CAN AN EMPLOYEE TAKE?

## AMOUNT OF LEAVE

Under the FMLA, an eligible employee is entitled to a total of 12 work-weeks of leave during any 12-month period. The employer is permitted to choose any one of the methods described below for determining the 12-month period in which the 12 weeks of leave entitlement occurs. If an employer fails to select one of these methods, the option that provides the most beneficial outcome for the employee will be used.

### The Calendar Year

If the employer chooses to use a calendar year, an employee would be entitled to up to 12 weeks of FMLA leave at any time during the calendar year. An employee could, therefore, take 12 weeks of leave at the end of the calendar year and 12 weeks at the beginning of the following calendar year.

### Any Fixed 12-Month Leave Year

An employer may choose to use any fixed 12-month leave year, such as (1) a fiscal year; (2) a year required by State law; or (3) a year starting on an employee's anniversary date of employment. In this case, an employee would be entitled to up to 12 weeks of FMLA leave at any time during the fixed 12-month leave year. An employee could, therefore, take 12 weeks of leave at the end of the fixed 12-month leave year and 12 weeks at the beginning of the following fixed 12-month leave year.

### The 12-Month Period From the Date of the Employee's First FMLA Leave

An employer may choose to use the 12-month period measured forward from the date an employee's first FMLA leave begins. In this case, an employee would be entitled to 12 weeks of leave during the year beginning on the first date FMLA leave is taken, and the next 12-month period would begin the first time FMLA leave is taken after completion of any previous 12-month period.

An employer may choose to use a rolling 12-month period measured backward from the date an employee uses any FMLA leave. In this case, each time an employee takes FMLA leave, the remaining leave entitlement would be any balance of the 12 weeks that had not been used during the immediately preceding 12 months.

### UNIFORMITY REQUIREMENT

The employer's chosen method must be applied consistently and uniformly to all employees. If the employer wants to change to another method, 60 days notice must be given to all employees, and the employees must be given their full benefit of 12 weeks of leave under whichever method affords the greatest benefit to the employee. At the conclusion of the 60-day period, the employer may implement the selected option.

### MULTI-STATE EMPLOYER EXCEPTION

There is an exception to the uniformity requirement described above in the case of a multi-State employer who has eligible employees in a State which has a family and medical leave statute. For example, the State may require a single method of determining the period during which use of the leave entitlement is measured which may conflict with the employer's chosen method. Under this scenario, the employer may comply with the State provision for all employees employed within that State, and uniformly use the employer's chosen method for all other employees.

### HOLIDAYS AND CLOSURES

If a holiday falls within the week an employee takes as FMLA leave, the week is still counted as a full week of FMLA leave. However, if the employer's business activity temporarily ceases for some reason—e.g. to make repairs—and the employees are not expected to work for one or more weeks, the days during which the employer's business activities were suspended do not count against an employee's FMLA leave entitlement. For school employees, this would include extended closures, such as spring and winter breaks and summer vacation periods.

### LEAVE FOR BIRTH OR PLACEMENT OF CHILD

An employee's leave entitlement for the birth of a baby or the placement of a child for adoption or foster care expires at the end of the 12-month period beginning on the date of the birth or placement, unless state law allows, or the employer permits, leave to be taken for a longer period. Thus, the 12 workweeks of FMLA leave to which the employee is entitled must be concluded within this one-year period.

## LEAVE ENTITLEMENT FOR HUSBAND AND WIFE WITH SAME EMPLOYER

Under the FMLA, a husband and wife who are eligible for FMLA leave and employed by the same covered employer may be limited to a combined total of 12 weeks of leave during any 12-month period if the leave is taken: (1) for the birth of the employees' son or daughter or to care for the newborn baby; (2) for placement of a son or daughter with the employees for adoption or foster care, or to care for the child after placement; or (3) to care for the employee's parent with a serious health condition.

The limitation on total leave time by a husband and wife employed by the same employer would apply even though the spouses are employed at two different worksites or divisions of the employer. However, if one spouse were ineligible for FMLA leave, the other spouse would be entitled to the full 12 workweeks of FMLA leave.

In addition, if the husband and wife both use a portion of the total 12-week FMLA leave entitlement for one of the purposes set forth above, the husband and wife would each then be entitled to the difference between the amount of leave taken individually, and the full 12 weeks for FMLA leave for a qualifying reason other than those described above. For example, if each spouse took 6 weeks to care for their newborn baby, they are each individually entitled to an additional 6 weeks of FMLA leave if needed to care for a parent with a serious health condition.

The reader is advised to check the law of his or her own state to determine whether any additional benefits apply. For example, many state disability laws allow for a period of disability for a pregnant woman prior to the birth of the baby. This period of disability would also be considered FMLA leave for a serious health condition of the mother, but would not be subject to the combined limit for both husband and wife. In addition, an employee may be entitled to additional non-FMLA leave under state law.

## INTERMITTENT LEAVE AND THE REDUCED LEAVE SCHEDULE

Under certain circumstances, FMLA leave may be taken intermittently or on a reduced leave schedule. Intermittent leave is FMLA leave taken in separate blocks of time due to a single qualifying reason. A reduced leave schedule is a leave schedule that reduces an employee's usual number of working hours per workweek, or hours per workday, thus a reduced leave schedule is a change in the employee's schedule for a period of time from full-time to part-time.

To qualify for intermittent leave, or leave on a reduced leave schedule, there must be a medical need for the requested leave that is best accommodated through an intermittent or reduced leave schedule. In addition, the employee who needs an intermittent or reduced leave schedule must attempt to schedule their leave so as not to disrupt the employer's business operations.

In such a situation, the employer is permitted to assign the employee to an alternative position with equivalent pay and benefits that better accommodates the employee's intermittent or reduced leave schedule, however, the alternative position does not have to have equivalent duties. In addition, the employer may increase the pay and benefits of an existing alternative position, so as to make them equivalent to the pay and benefits of the employee's regular job. An employer may not transfer the employee to an alternative position in order to discourage the employee from taking FMLA leave.

Special rules apply depending on the reason intermittent leave or a reduced leave schedule is requested, as discussed below.

### Birth or Placement of Child

When FMLA leave is taken after the birth or placement of a child, an employee may take leave intermittently or on a reduced leave schedule only if the employer agrees to the arrangement. The employer's agreement is not required, however, for FMLA leave taken due to the mother's serious health condition in connection with the birth of her child, or if the newborn child has a serious health condition.

### Continuous Medical Treatment and Recovery Time

Intermittent leave or a reduced leave schedule is permitted when medically necessary for planned and/or unanticipated medical treatment of a related serious health condition by or under the supervision of a health care provider, or for recovery from treatment, or recovery from a serious health condition. It may also be taken to provide care or psychological comfort to an immediate family member with a serious health condition, or the employee is needed to fill in for other caregivers or make arrangements for the care of the family member with a serious health condition.

Intermittent or reduced schedule leave may also be taken for absences where the employee is unable to perform the essential functions of their job because of a chronic serious health condition, even if the employee does not receive treatment by a health care provider.

### Periodic Medical Treatment

Intermittent or reduced schedule leave may be taken for a serious health condition which requires treatment by a health care provider periodically, rather than for one continuous period of time, and may include leave of periods from an hour or more—e.g., for medical appointments—to several weeks.

### Limitations on Size of Leave Increments

There is no limit on the size of an increment of leave an employee may take intermittently or on a reduced leave schedule. For example, an employee might take two hours off for a medical appointment, or might work a reduced day of four hours over a period of several weeks while recuperating from an illness.

### Special Rules for Instructional Employees

If an eligible instructional employee needs intermittent leave or leave on a reduced leave schedule to care for a family member, or for the employee's own serious health condition, which is foreseeable because it is based on planned medical treatment, and the employee would be on leave for more than 20 percent of the total number of working days over the period the leave would extend, the employer may require the employee to choose either to:

1. Take leave for a period or periods of a particular duration, not greater than the duration of the planned treatment; or

2. Transfer temporarily to an available alternative position for which the employee is qualified, which has equivalent pay and benefits and which better accommodates recurring periods of leave than does the employee's regular position.

These rules apply only to a leave involving more than 20 percent of the working days during the period over which the leave extends. For example, if an instructional employee who normally works five days each week needs to take two days of FMLA leave per week over a period of several weeks, the special rules would apply. Employees taking leave which constitutes 20 percent or less of the working days during the leave period would not be subject to transfer to an alternative position.

If an instructional employee does not give required notice of foreseeable FMLA leave to be taken intermittently or on a reduced leave schedule, the employer may require the employee to take leave of a particular duration, or to transfer temporarily to an alternative position. Alternatively, the employer may require the employee to delay the taking of leave until the notice provision is met.

If the instructional employee takes FMLA leave for a period that ends with the school year and begins the next semester, this is considered leave taken consecutively rather than intermittently. The period during the summer vacation when the employee would not have been required to report for duty is not counted against the employee's FMLA leave entitlement. In addition, an instructional employee who is on FMLA leave at the end of the school year must be provided with any benefits over the summer vacation that employees would normally receive if they had been working at the end of the school year.

There are also different rules for instructional employees who begin leave more than five weeks before the end of a term, less than five weeks before the end of a term, and less than three weeks before the end of a term, as follows:

1. If an instructional employee begins leave more than five weeks before the end of a term, the employer may require the employee to continue taking leave until the end of the term if: (a) The leave will last at least three weeks; and (b) The employee would return to work during the three-week period before the end of the term.

2. If the employee begins leave for a purpose other than the employee's own serious health condition during the five-week period before the end of a term, the employer may require the employee to continue taking leave until the end of the term if: (a) the leave will last more than two weeks; and (b) the employee would return to work during the two-week period before the end of the term.

3. If the employee begins leave for a purpose other than the employee's own serious health condition during the three-week period before the end of a term, and the leave will last more than five working days, the employer may require the employee to continue taking leave until the end of the term.

It should be noted, however, that where the employer requires the employee to take leave until the end of an academic term, only the period of leave until the employee is ready and able to return to work will be charged against the employee's FMLA leave entitlement. This is because the employer has the option not to require the employee to stay on leave until the end of the school term. Therefore, any additional leave required by the employer to the end of the school term is not counted as FMLA leave. Nevertheless, the employer is still required to maintain the employee's group health insurance and other benefits, and restore the employee to the same or equivalent job, at the conclusion of the employee's leave.

## SUBSTITUTION RULES

Generally, FMLA leave is unpaid. However, under certain circumstances, the FMLA permits an eligible employee to choose to substitute paid leave for FMLA leave. If an employee does not choose to substitute accrued paid leave, the employer may require the employee to substitute accrued paid leave for FMLA leave.

### Paid Medical Leave

Substitution of paid medical leave may be elected to the extent the circumstances meet the employer's usual requirements for the use of medical leave. However, an employer is not required to allow substitution of paid medical leave for unpaid FMLA leave in situations where the employer's uniform policy would not normally allow such paid leave.

An employee, therefore, has a right to substitute paid medical leave to care for a seriously ill family member only if the employer's leave plan allows paid leave to be used for that purpose.

Similarly, an employee does not have a right to substitute paid medical leave for a serious health condition that is not covered by the employer's leave plan.

### Paid Vacation or Personal Leave

Paid vacation or personal leave may be substituted, at either the employee's or the employer's option, for any qualified FMLA leave. No limitations may be placed by the employer on substitution of paid vacation or personal leave for these purposes.

However, if an employee uses paid leave under circumstances which do not qualify as FMLA leave, the leave will not count against the 12 weeks of FMLA leave to which the employee is entitled. For example, paid sick leave used for a medical condition that is not a serious health condition does not count against the 12 weeks of FMLA leave entitlement.

### Designating Leave as FMLA Leave

It is the employer's responsibility to designate leave, paid or unpaid, as FMLA-covered, and to give notice of the designation to the employee. The employer's designation decision must be based only on information received from the employee or the employee's representative. Once the employer is aware that the leave is being taken for an FMLA-covered reason, the employer must notify the employee within two business days that the paid leave is being designated and counted as FMLA leave.

The employer's notice to the employee that the leave has been designated as FMLA leave may be made orally or in writing. If the notice is oral, it must be confirmed in writing no later than the following payday. The written notice may be in any form, including a notation on the employee's pay stub.

If the employer learns that leave is for an FMLA purpose after leave has already begun, the entire amount, or some portion, of the paid leave period may be retroactively counted as FMLA leave, to the extent that the leave period qualified as FMLA leave.

Employers may not designate leave as FMLA leave after the employee has returned to work with two exceptions:

1. If the employee was absent for an FMLA reason and the employer did not learn the reason for the absence until the employee's return, the employer may, within two business days of the employee's return to work, designate the leave retroactively with appropriate notice to the employee.

2. If the employer knows the reason for the leave but has not been able to confirm that the leave qualifies under FMLA, or where the employer has requested medical certification which has not yet been received, the employer should make a preliminary designation, and notify the employee at the time leave begins, or as soon as the reason for the leave becomes known. Upon receipt of the information from the employee or of the medical certification that confirms the leave is for an FMLA reason, the preliminary designation becomes final. If the medical certification fails to confirm that the reason for the absence was an FMLA reason, the employer must withdraw the designation, with written notice to the employee.

# CHAPTER 6:
# MEDICAL CERTIFICATION REQUIREMENT

## IN GENERAL

When an employee requests FMLA leave due to his or her own serious health condition, or the serious health condition of an immediate family member, the employer may require the employee to provide medical certification to support his or her request for FMLA leave.

To comply with this requirement, the employee must provide a detailed medical certification form prepared by the employee's health care provider or the health care provider for the employee's family member. The medical certification must confirm that a serious health condition exists. However, an employee is not required to provide medical records to their employer.

If the employer's sick or medical leave plan imposes medical certification requirements that are less stringent than the FMLA certification requirements, and the employee or employer elects to substitute paid sick, vacation, personal or family leave for unpaid FMLA leave, the employer's less stringent sick leave certification requirements must be followed instead of the FMLA certification requirements.

## MEDICAL CERTIFICATION FORM

The information contained on the medical certification form must relate only to the serious health condition of the employee or the employee's immediate family member for which the need for FMLA leave exists. The form must contain the following information:

1. The health care provider's identifying information;

2. The health care provider's type of medical practice and any pertinent specialization;

3. A certification as to which part of the FMLA definition of "serious health condition" applies to the patient's condition, and the medical

facts which support the certification, including a brief statement as to how the medical facts meet the criteria of the definition.

4. The approximate date the serious health condition began, and its probable duration, including the probable duration of the patient's present incapacity;

5. Whether it will be necessary for the employee to take leave intermittently or to work on a reduced leave schedule basis as a result of the serious health condition and, if so, the probable duration of such schedule.

6. If the condition is pregnancy or a chronic condition, the form must state whether the patient is presently incapacitated, and the likely duration and frequency of episodes of incapacity.

7. The form must state whether additional treatments will be required for the condition, and provide an estimate of the probable number of such treatments.

8. If the patient's incapacity will be intermittent, or will require a reduced leave schedule, the form must provide an estimate of the probable number of treatments; the interval between such treatments; the actual or estimated dates of treatment, if known; and the period required for recovery, if any.

9. If any of the treatments will be provided by another health care provider, the form must describe the nature of those treatments.

10. If a regimen of continuing treatment by the patient is required under the supervision of the health care provider, the form must provide a general description of that regimen.

11. If the employee is requesting medical leave because of the employee's own condition, the form must state:

(a) Whether the employee is unable to perform work of any kind;

(b) Whether the employee is unable to perform any one or more of the essential functions of the employee's position. This should include a statement describing the essential functions of the employee's position based on a statement provided by the employer or information provided by the employee.

(c) Whether the employee must be absent from work for treatment.

12. If the employee is requesting leave to care for a family member with a serious health condition, the form must state:

(a) Whether the patient requires assistance for basic medical or personal needs or safety, or for transportation; or

(b) If not, whether the employee's presence to provide psychological comfort would be beneficial to the patient or assist in the patient's recovery.

(c) A description by the employee of the care he or she will provide and an estimate of the time period such care will be provided;

(d) Whether the employee's family member will only need care intermittently or on a reduced leave schedule basis and, if so, the probable duration of the need.

The Department of Labor has developed an optional form for employees' to use to obtain the required medical certification from their health care provider. DOL Form WH-380 meets all of the FMLA certification requirements, and permits the health care provider to furnish all of the appropriate medical information within his or her knowledge.

A copy of the Certification of Health Care Provider [DOL Form WH-380] is set forth at Appendix 3.

### WHEN MUST AN EMPLOYEE PROVIDE MEDICAL CERTIFICATION?

The medical certification requirement arises when the employee requests FMLA leave to care for the employee's immediate family member who has a serious health condition, or due to the employee's own serious health condition, as discussed in Chapter 4 of this almanac. If the employer requires medical certification, the employer must give the employee notice of the requirement each time a certification is required.

In most cases, where the leave is foreseeable, and the employee provides at least 30 days notice of the need for leave, the employer's request for medical certification should be made at the time the employee gives notice of the need for leave, or within two business days thereafter. The employee should provide the medical certification before the leave begins. When this is not possible, the employee must provide the requested certification to the employer within the time requested by the employer, but no sooner than 15 days after the employer's request, unless the employee is unable to comply despite his or her diligent, good faith effort to do so. In the case of unforeseen leave, the employer's request for medical certification should be made within two business days after the employee's leave commences.

At the time the employer requests certification, the employer must also advise an employee of the anticipated consequences of an employee's failure to provide adequate certification.

### INCOMPLETE OR INADEQUATE MEDICAL CERTIFICATION FORMS

If the employer finds that a certification is incomplete, he must notify the employee and provide the employee a reasonable opportunity to cure the deficiency. If an employee submits a complete certification signed by the health care provider, the employer may not request additional information from the employee's health care provider. However, a health care provider representing the employer may contact the employee's health care provider, with the employee's permission, for purposes of clarification and authenticity of the medical certification.

If an employee is on FMLA leave at the same time he or she is on a workers' compensation absence, and the provisions of the workers' compensation statute permit the employer or the employer's representative to have direct contact with the employee's workers' compensation health care provider, the employer has the right to follow the workers' compensation provisions regarding direct contact.

### SECOND OPINION

If an employer has reason to doubt the validity of a medical certification, the employer may require the employee to obtain a second opinion at the employer's expense. The employer is permitted to designate the health care provider to furnish the second opinion, however, the selected health care provider may not be employed on a regular basis by the employer.

While waiting for the results of the second medical opinion, the employee is entitled to all of the FMLA benefits, including maintenance of group health benefits. However, if the certification does not ultimately support the employee's right to FMLA leave, the leave shall not be designated as FMLA leave. In that case, the employer may treat the leave as either paid or unpaid leave according to the employer's leave policies.

### THIRD OPINION

If the opinions of the employee's and the employer's respective health care providers differ, the employer may require the employee to obtain certification from a third health care provider, again at the employer's expense. This third opinion shall be final and binding.

The third health care provider must be designated or approved by both the employer and the employee. There must be a good faith effort by both parties to choose the third health care provider. If the employer does not attempt in good faith to reach an agreement, the employer will be bound by the first certification. If the employee does not attempt in good faith to reach an agreement, the employee will be bound by the second certification.

If the employer requires a second or third opinion, the employer must reimburse the employee or family member for any reasonable "out of pocket" travel expenses incurred in obtaining the second and third medical opinions. Nevertheless, the employer may not require the employee or family member to travel outside a normal commuting distance for purposes of obtaining the second or third medical opinion except in very unusual circumstances.

## TRAVEL OUTSIDE THE UNITED STATES

If the employee, or the employee's immediate family member is traveling outside the United States, or the immediate family member resides in another country, and a serious health condition develops, the employer shall accept a medical certification, and a second and third opinion, if required, from a health care provider who practices in that country.

## RECERTIFICATION

Under certain circumstances, the employer may request additional medical certification at some later date, as discussed below. Any recertification requested by the employer shall be at the employee's expense unless the employer provides otherwise. No second or third opinion on recertification may be required.

If an employee is pregnant, or suffers from a chronic, or permanent/long-term condition, and is under the continuing supervision of a health care provider, an employer may request recertification no more often than every 30 days, and only in connection with an absence by the employee. If the certification states that the patient's incapacity will exceed 30 days, or the employee's FMLA leave is taken intermittently or on a reduced leave schedule basis, the employer may not request recertification until the minimum duration has passed.

### Exceptions

The employer does not have to comply with the time limit on a recertification request if:

1. Circumstances described by the previous certification have changed significantly, e.g., the duration or frequency of absences; or

2. The employer receives information that casts doubt upon the employee's stated reason for the absence; or

3. The employee requests an extension of leave.

The employee must provide the requested recertification to the employer within the time frame requested by the employer, but no sooner than 15 days after the employer's request. An exception exists if it is not practicable under the particular circumstances for the employee to provide the recertification within this time period despite the employee's diligent, good faith efforts.

## FITNESS-FOR-DUTY CERTIFICATION

Under certain circumstances, as a condition of restoring an employee to his or her former position, an employer may require the employee to submit a medical certification that he or she is fit for duty and able to return to work, as follows:

1. If an employee takes FMLA leave for a serious health condition that made him or her unable to perform their job. However, the policy must be applied uniformly among employees who are "similarly situated"—i.e., same occupation and same serious health condition.

2. If State or local law, or the terms of a collective bargaining agreement, govern an employee's return to work, those provisions must be followed.

3. An employer is not entitled to a fitness-for-duty certification when the employee takes intermittent leave.

Under the Americans with Disabilities Act (ADA), any fitness-for-duty physical must be job-related, i.e., the examination and certification must relate to the essential functions of the employee's job. Further, an employer may only request a fitness-for-duty certification in connection with the serious health condition that caused the employee's need for FMLA leave.

### Notice Requirement

An employer is required to advise employees whether a fitness-for-duty certification will be required. The employer's policy should be contained in the employment handbook, if any.

Specific notice must also be given to any employee from whom fitness-for-duty certification will be required, either at the time notice of the need for leave is given, or immediately after leave begins, and the employer is advised of the employee's medical circumstances. An employer may delay the employee's return to work until the required fitness-for-duty certification is provided, unless the employer failed to provide notice of the policy.

### Content

The fitness-for-duty certification is merely a statement by the employee's health care provider that the employee is able to return to work and perform the functions of his or her job. Further, the employer is entitled to have a health care provider employed by the employer contact the employee's health care provider, with the employee's permission, to clarify the employee's ability to return to work. However, the employer's health care provider may only request clarification related to the serious health condition that caused the employee's need for FMLA leave.

### Cost

The employee is responsible for the cost of obtaining the fitness-for-duty certification, including any associated costs.

### FAILURE TO SATISFY MEDICAL CERTIFICATION REQUIREMENTS

If an employee fails to satisfy any of the medical certification and/or recertification requirements discussed above within the applicable time period, he or she is subject to the following actions by the employer:

1. If the leave is foreseeable, an employer may delay the employee's FMLA leave until the medical certification is provided.

2. If the need for leave is not foreseeable—e.g., a medical emergency—and the employee fails to provide the medical certification within a reasonable time period under the circumstances, the employer may delay the employee's continuation of FMLA leave.

3. If the employee fails to provide any medical certification, the employee's leave time will not be deemed FMLA leave.

4. If the employee fails to provide a fitness-for-duty certification, where required, the employee may be terminated at the time the FMLA leave is concluded.

# CHAPTER 7:
# JOB PROTECTION

### IN GENERAL

One of the most important provisions of the FMLA is job protection. Thus, when an employee returns from FMLA leave, he or she is entitled to be returned to the same position the employee held when leave began, or to an equivalent position with equivalent benefits, pay, and other terms and conditions of employment. An employee is entitled to reinstatement even if the employee has been replaced or his or her position has been restructured to accommodate the employee's absence.

Under the FMLA, if the employee is unable to perform an essential function of his or her former position because of a physical or mental condition, the employee has no right to return to another position. However, the employee may have some recourse under the Americans with Disabilities Act (ADA).

### WHAT IS AN EQUIVALENT POSITION?

An equivalent position is one that is virtually identical to the employee's former position in terms of pay, benefits and working conditions, including privileges and status. In addition, the position must involve the same or substantially similar duties and responsibilities as the employee's former position, and must entail equivalent skill, effort, responsibility, and authority.

Upon return from FMLA leave, the employee must be reinstated to the same worksite, or a worksite that is in close proximity to the one where the employee had previously been employed. If the employee's original worksite has been closed, the employee is entitled to the same rights as if the employee had not been on leave when the worksite closed.

For example, if an employer transfers all employees from a closed worksite to a new worksite in a different city, the employee returning from FMLA leave is also entitled to transfer under the same conditions as if he or she had not been on leave at the time of the transfer.

An employee is also generally entitled to return to the same shift or work schedule as their original position. However, if the employee's former shift was eliminated while the employee was on FMLA leave, the employee is not entitled to return to work that same shift.

The FMLA does not prohibit an employer from granting an employee's request to be restored to a different shift, schedule, or position which better suits the employee's personal needs upon their return from FMLA leave. Nevertheless, an employee cannot be induced by the employer to accept a different position against the employee's wishes.

If as a result of taking FMLA leave, an employee is no longer qualified for his or her former position because of the employee's inability to fulfill certain conditions of the job—e.g., the employee failed to renew a required license while on FMLA leave—the employee must be given a reasonable opportunity to fulfill those conditions upon his or her return to work.

### WHAT IS EQUIVALENT PAY?

An employee is entitled to any unconditional pay increases which may have occurred while he or she was on FMLA leave, such as a cost of living increase. However, pay increases based on seniority, length of service, or work performed would not have to be granted unless it is the employer's policy to do so for other employees who are out on unpaid leave. If so, an employee is entitled to any pay increases that would have been granted on these bases while the employee was on FMLA leave.

### WHAT ARE EQUIVALENT BENEFITS?

Employee benefits include all of the benefits provided to employees, such as group life insurance, health insurance, disability insurance, sick leave, annual leave, educational benefits, and pensions. At the end of an employee's FMLA leave, these benefits must be resumed in the same manner as provided when the leave began, and an employee cannot be required to requalify for any benefits the employee was entitled to before FMLA leave began.

An employee may, but is not entitled to, accrue any additional benefits or seniority during their unpaid FMLA leave. However, benefits accrued at the time leave began, such as paid vacation, sick or personal leave, must be available to an employee upon return from leave, provided those benefits were not substituted for unpaid FMLA leave.

## RETIREMENT AND PENSION PLANS

Any period of unpaid FMLA leave taken by an employee cannot be counted as a break in service for purposes of vesting and eligibility to participate in any retirement and pension plan. Thus, if the plan requires an employee to be employed on a specific date in order to be credited with a year of service for vesting, contributions or participation purposes, an employee on unpaid FMLA leave on that date shall be deemed to have been employed on that date.

## LIMITATIONS ON THE EMPLOYEE'S RIGHT TO REINSTATEMENT

It must be noted that an employee has no greater right to reinstatement or to other benefits and conditions of employment than if the employee had been continuously employed during the FMLA leave period. However, an employer must be able to show that the employee would not otherwise have been employed at the time reinstatement is requested in order to deny restoration to employment.

For example, if an employee was hired for a specific term, or to work on a specific project, and the term or project is completed by the time the employee's FMLA leave ends, the employer is not obligated to continue to employ that employee.

### Key Employees

A "key employee" is a salaried FMLA-eligible employee who is among the highest paid 10 percent of all the employees working for the employer within 75 miles of the worksite. An employer is not obligated to restore a key employee to his or her former position if it will cause substantial and grievous economic injury to the employer's business.

In making this determination, an employer may take into account its ability to either do without the employee during his or her FMLA leave, or replace the employee on a temporary basis. If permanent replacement is unavoidable, then the cost of reinstating the employee may be considered in evaluating the extent of economic injury that the employer will suffer if he restores the employee to his or her former or equivalent position.

If the employer believes that reinstatement of a key employee may be denied, the employer must give the key employee written notice of his or her status as a key employee at the time the employee requests FMLA leave, or when FMLA leave commences, whichever occurs first. The employer must advise the employee of the potential consequences regarding reinstatement and maintenance of benefits if the employer determines that reinstatement will cause a substantial and grievous economic injury to the employer's business operations. An employer who fails to provide such timely notice will lose its right to deny restoration to the key employee, even if substantial and grievous economic injury will result from reinstatement.

As soon as the employer makes a good faith determination that substantial and grievous economic injury will result from reinstatement of the key employee who requests FMLA leave, the employer must notify the employee in writing that, although it cannot deny FMLA leave, the employer intends to deny reinstatement when the key employee's FMLA leave is over.

Notice must be in writing and served on the employee in person or by certified mail, and must explain the basis for the employer's determination. If FMLA leave has already begun, the employer must provide the employee with a reasonable time in which to return to work. If the employee does not return to work in response to the employer's notification of intent to deny restoration, the employee continues to be entitled to maintenance of health benefits while on FMLA leave.

The key employee is still entitled to request reinstatement at the end of their FMLA leave period even if the employee received the employer's written notice and did not return to work. At that time, the employer must again determine whether there will be substantial and grievous economic injury to the business if the employer reinstates the key employee. If it is again determined that substantial and grievous economic injury will result, the employer must again notify the employee in writing of the denial of restoration.

## ALTERNATIVE POSITIONS

If an employee needs intermittent leave or leave on a reduced leave schedule that is foreseeable based on planned medical treatment for the employee or a family member, or if the employer agrees to permit intermittent or reduced schedule leave for the birth of a child or for placement of a child for adoption or foster care, the employer may require the employee to transfer temporarily to an available alternative position during the period the intermittent or reduced leave schedule is required.

In this case, the employee must be qualified for the alternative position, and the position must better accommodate the employee's intermittent or reduced leave schedule. In addition, the alternative position must have equivalent pay and benefits, but does not have to have equivalent duties. The employer may increase the pay and benefits of an existing alternative position, so as to make the position equivalent to the pay and benefits of the employee's original position.

The employer may also transfer the employee to a part-time job with the same hourly rate of pay and benefits, provided the employee is not required to take more leave than is medically necessary by working part-time hours. For example, an employee who requests a reduced leave schedule of four hours per day could be transferred to a half-time position that has the same benefits and pays the same hourly rate as the employee's original job. Once the employee's need for FMLA leave is over, the employee must be reinstated to a full-time position.

An employer is prohibited from transferring an employee to an alternative position as a tactic for discouraging the employee from taking leave or causing the employee hardship. For example, a white-collar employee may not be assigned to a blue-collar position.

## MAINTAINING GROUP HEALTH PLAN BENEFITS

During FMLA leave, an employer must maintain the employee's coverage under any group health plan on the same conditions as coverage would have been provided if the employee had been continuously employed during the entire leave period. In addition, if an employer provides a new health plan or benefits or changes health benefits or plans while an employee is on FMLA leave, the employee is entitled to the new or changed benefits to the same extent as if the employee were not on leave.

For example, if an employer changes a group health plan so that dental care becomes covered under the plan, an employee on FMLA leave must be given the same opportunity as other employees to obtain dental care coverage. Likewise, any other plan changes, including changes in coverage, premiums, and deductibles, etc., which apply to all employees, also apply to an employee on FMLA leave.

While an employee is on FMLA leave, he or she is still obligated to pay any share of group health plan premiums which the employee was obligated to pay prior to taking FMLA leave. If the FMLA leave is substituted paid leave, the employee's share of premiums will continue to be paid as usual, e.g. by payroll deduction. If the FMLA leave is unpaid, the employer may require that the employee make payment to the employer or to the insurance carrier. The employer may require employees to pay their share of premium payments in any of the following ways:

1. Payment due at the same time as it would be made if by payroll deduction;

2. Payment due on the same schedule as payments are made under COBRA;

3. The employer's existing rules for payment by employees on leave without pay would be followed; or

4. A system agreed to between the employer and the employee.

If an employee fails to make timely health plan premium payments, the employer is no longer obligated to maintain health insurance coverage under the FMLA. The FMLA permits the employer to end coverage if the employee's premium payment is more than 30 days late, although an employer may provide a longer grace period for payment of the premium.

In order to drop health care coverage for an employee whose premium payment is late, the employer must provide written notice to the employee that the payment has not been received. The required notice must be mailed to the employee at least 15 days before coverage is to cease. The notice must advise the employee that coverage will be dropped on a specified date at least 15 days after the date of the letter, unless the payment has been received by that date.

If the employee's group health plan coverage lapses because the employee has not made the required premium payments, the employer must still restore the employee's benefits upon the employee's return from FMLA leave.

If the employee fails to return following the FMLA leave period, the employer is entitled to recover its share of health plan premiums paid during the employee's FMLA leave, unless the reason the employee does not return is due to:

1. The continuation, recurrence, or onset of a serious health condition of the employee or the employee's family member which would otherwise entitle the employee to leave under the FMLA; or

2. Other circumstances beyond the employee's control, e.g., the employee's spouse was unexpectedly transferred out of the area; a family member other than an immediate family member has a serious health condition and the employee is needed to provide care; or the employee is laid off while on leave, etc.

The health plan premiums an employer is permitted to recover are considered a debt owed by the non-returning employee to the employer. The employer may recover the costs through deduction from any sums due to the employee, e.g., unpaid wages, vacation pay, etc. Alternatively, the employer may initiate legal action against the employee to recover the costs of the health plan premiums.

# CHAPTER 8:
# EMPLOYER RESPONSIBILITIES

## NOTICE REQUIREMENTS

Under the FMLA, every covered employer is obligated to make sure its workforce is aware of the FMLA and its provisions. Notice requirements are discussed below.

### Posting the Notice

Every employer covered by the FMLA is required to post a notice on the premises of the business which explains the FMLA and its provisions. The notice must be posted in a conspicuous and prominent place where employees as well as applicants are likely to view it. The required notice must be posted whether or not the employer has FMLA-eligible employees. The notice must provide information explaining the procedures an employee must follow in order to file a complaint against employers who violate the FMLA. Further, if a significant number of the employer's workers are non-English speaking, the employer must also post the notice in a language in which employees are literate. The posted notice and text must be large enough so that it is legible and easy to read.

The Department of Labor has designed a poster that meets these requirements. Copies of the poster may be obtained from the Department of Labor, Wage and Hour Division. Alternatively, the employer may duplicate the text of the notice.

A copy of the poster "Your Rights Under the Family and Medical Leave Act of 1993" is set forth at Appendix 4.

An employer that willfully violates the notice requirement may be assessed a civil monetary penalty. Presently, the monetary penalty cannot exceed $100 for each separate violation. In addition, any employer who fails to post the required notice cannot take any adverse action against an employee who fails to provide the employer with advance notice of the employee's need to take FMLA leave. For example, the employer cannot deny the employee's request for FMLA leave.

### Written Guidelines

If an employer covered by the FMLA has any eligible employees, and has any written guidelines for its employees, such as an employee handbook, which discusses employee benefits and/or leave rights, information concerning the employees' rights under the FMLA must be included. If the employer does not have an employee handbook or manual, the employer must provide employees with written notice of the employees' rights under the FMLA. The employer is also required to respond to any questions the employees may have concerning FMLA leave.

The required written notice must be in the language in which the employees are literate. The notice should discuss the employer's FMLA policies, the employee's rights and obligations under the law, and any consequences an employee may suffer for failing to comply with the FMLA requirements, including:

1. Whether the leave will be counted against the employee's annual FMLA leave entitlement;

2. Any requirements for the employee to furnish medical certification of a serious health condition and the consequences of failing to do so;

3. The employee's right to substitute paid leave for FMLA leave;

4. Whether the employer will require the substitution of paid leave;

5. Any conditions related to substitution of paid leave for FMLA leave;

6. Whether there is a requirement for the employee to make any premium payments to maintain health benefits and, if so, the arrangements for making such payments;

7. The potential consequences of the employee's failure to make any required premium payments on a timely basis, such as lapse in coverage;

8. Whether there is a requirement for the employee to provide a fitness-for-duty certificate to be restored to employment at the end of the FMLA leave period;

9. The employee's status as a 'key employee' and the potential consequence that restoration may be denied a key employee following FMLA leave, and an explanation of the circumstances under which such a denial may be made;

10. The employee's right to restoration to the same or an equivalent job upon return from FMLA leave;

11. The employee's potential liability for payment of health insurance premiums paid by the employer during the employee's unpaid FMLA leave if the employee fails to return to work after taking FMLA leave; and

12. Whether the employer will require periodic reports of the employee's status and intent to return to work.

The required written notice must be provided to an employee the first time in each six-month period that an employee gives notice of his or her need for FMLA leave. The notice must be given within a reasonable time—i.e., within one to two business days—after the employee gives the employer notice of the need for FMLA leave. If the employee's FMLA leave has already begun, the notice should be mailed to the employee's address of record.

If an employer fails to provide written notice to employees as discussed above, the employer is prohibited from subsequently taking any adverse action against an employee who fails to comply with any of the provisions which are required to be set forth in the written notice.

## RECORDKEEPING

Under the FMLA, a covered employer is required to maintain all records pertaining to their obligations under the law for no less than three years. The employer must make those records available for inspection, copying and transcription by Department of Labor (DOL) representatives upon request. The DOL is authorized to inspect the employer's books one time during any 12-month period, unless the DOL has reason to believe the employer is violating the FMLA, or if the DOL is investigating a complaint against the employer.

### Required Records

Covered employers who have FMLA-eligible employees must maintain records that disclose the following:

1. Basic employee payroll and identification information, including name, address, and occupation; rate or basis of pay and terms of compensation; daily and weekly hours worked per pay period; additions to or deductions from wages; and total compensation paid;

2. Dates FMLA leave is taken by FMLA-eligible employees. Leave must be designated in records as FMLA leave, and may not include leave required under State law or an employer plan which is not also covered by the FMLA;

3. If FMLA leave is taken by eligible employees in increments of less than one full day, the records must designate the hours of the leave taken;

4. Copies of employee notices of leave furnished to the employer under the FMLA, if in writing;

5. Copies of all general and specific written notices given to employees as required under the FMLA;

6. Any documents describing employee benefits or employer policies and practices regarding the taking of paid and unpaid leave;

7. Records relating to premium payments of employee benefits; and

8. Records of any dispute between the employer and an FMLA-eligible employee regarding designation of leave as FMLA leave, including any written statement from the employer or employee of the reasons for the designation and for the disagreement.

Covered employers who do not have any eligible employees are only required to keep records relating to employee payroll and identification information, as set forth above.

### Confidentiality of Records

Records and documents relating to medical certifications, re-certifications or medical histories of employees or employees' family members, created for FMLA purposes, must be maintained as confidential medical records. The records must be kept separately from the employee's personnel file. The following use of confidential records is permitted:

1. Supervisors and managers may be informed regarding necessary restrictions on the work or duties of an employee and necessary accommodations;

2. First aid and safety personnel may be informed if the employee's physical or medical condition might require emergency treatment; and

3. Government officials investigating compliance with the FMLA shall be provided relevant information upon request.

# CHAPTER 9:
# EMPLOYEE RESPONSIBILITIES

## NOTICE OF THE NEED FOR FMLA LEAVE

An employee is obligated to provide notice to his or her employer that the employee needs to take FMLA leave. The notice requirements differ according to whether the need for FMLA leave is foreseeable or unforeseeable, as further discussed below.

### Foreseeable Leave

If an employee needs to take FMLA leave, and the employee's need for leave is foreseeable, the employee must provide the employer at least 30 days advance notice before FMLA leave is to begin. Foreseeable leave includes circumstances such as an expected birth or placement of a son or daughter for adoption or foster care; elective surgery; or planned medical treatment for a serious health condition of the employee or the employee's immediate relative. When planning medical treatment, the employee must consult with the employer and make a reasonable effort to schedule the FMLA leave so as not to unduly disrupt the employer's business operations.

If a 30 day notice is not practicable, notice must be given as soon as practicable, i.e., as soon as possible and practical taking into account all of the facts and circumstances of the individual employee's situation. For example, due to a change in a pregnant employee's health condition, the employee may need to begin FMLA leave earlier than anticipated.

An employer may also require an employee to comply with the employer's usual and customary notice and procedural requirements for requesting leave. For example, an employer may require that written notice set forth the reasons for the requested leave, the anticipated duration of the leave, and the anticipated start date of the leave. However, even if the employee fails to follow the employer's procedures, the employer is still not permitted to disallow or delay the employee's

FMLA leave if the employee gives the employer timely verbal or other notice.

If an employee needs to take medically necessary intermittent leave, or leave on a reduced leave schedule the employee must advise the employer of the reasons why this type of leave is medically necessary, and provide the employer with a schedule of treatment. The employee and employer must attempt to work out a schedule that meets the employee's needs without unduly disrupting the employer's business operations.

Despite the foregoing provisions, an employer may waive the FMLA notice requirements. Further, if a collective bargaining agreement, State law, or the employer's leave plan permits less advance notice than the FMLA notice requirements, the employer may not require employees to follow the stricter FMLA notice requirements.

### Unforeseeable Leave

If an employee's need for FMLA leave is unforeseeable, the employee must give the employer notice of the need for FMLA leave as soon as practicable under the facts and circumstances of the individual employee's situation. This generally means that the employee should give notice to the employer within no more than one or two working days of learning of the need for leave, except in extraordinary circumstances where such notice is not feasible.

Notice may be given to the employer in person, or by telephone, telegraph, fax, or other electronic means. In addition, notice may be given by the employee's representative—such as a spouse, adult family member or other responsible party—if the employee is unable to do so personally. This may occur, for example, if the employee is unconscious.

### What Happens if an Employee Fails to Give the Employer Notice?

In the case of foreseeable leave, if an employee fails to give the 30 day notice, with no reasonable excuse for the delay, the employer may delay the taking of FMLA leave until at least 30 days after the date the employee provides notice to the employer of the need for FMLA leave. However, the need for leave and the approximate date leave would be taken must have been clearly foreseeable to the employee 30 days in advance for this provision to apply.

In all cases, in order for the onset of an employee's FMLA leave to be delayed due to lack of required notice, it must be clear that the employee had actual notice of the FMLA notice requirements. This condition would be satisfied by the employer's proper posting of the required notice at the worksite where the employee is employed, as discussed in Chapter 8.

## NOTICE OF INTENT TO RETURN TO WORK

An employee on FMLA leave may be required to periodically report on his or her status and intent to return to work. However, the employer's policy regarding this reporting requirement must not be discriminatory, and must take into account all of the relevant facts and circumstances related to the individual employee's leave.

If the employee gives the employer unequivocal notice that the employee does not intend to return to work, the employer's obligations of maintaining health benefits, and restoring the employee to his or her former position, no longer apply.

## MEDICAL CERTIFICATION

As set forth in Chapter 6, an employer may require an employee to provide medical certification to support his or her request for FMLA leave. If the employee fails to provide the requested medical certification in a timely manner, an employer may delay continuation of FMLA leave until the employee submits the certificate. If the employee never produces the required medical certification, the leave is not FMLA leave. Likewise, if an employee fails to provide a requested fitness-for-duty certification to return to work, an employer may delay restoration until the employee submits the certificate.

If an employee fraudulently obtains FMLA leave from an employer, the employee is not protected by job restoration or maintenance of health benefits provisions under the FMLA.

# CHAPTER 10:
# ENFORCEMENT MEASURES

**WHAT RECOURSE DOES AN EMPLOYEE HAVE IF THEIR FMLA RIGHTS ARE VIOLATED?**

If an employee's rights under the FMLA are violated by his or her employer, the employee may:

1. File a complaint against their employer with the Secretary of Labor; or

2. File a private lawsuit against their employer.

If an employee decides to file a private lawsuit, it must be filed within two years after the last action which the employee contends was in violation of the FMLA, or three years if the violation was willful.

**RELIEF**

If it is shown that the employer violated one or more provisions of the FMLA, the employee may receive the wages, employment benefits, or other compensation that was denied or lost to the employee due to the violation.

If there was no tangible loss—e.g., when the violation was an unlawful denial of FMLA leave—the employee may recover any actual monetary loss suffered as a direct result of the violation. This may include the cost of providing care, up to a sum equal to 12 weeks of wages for the employee, with interest calculated at the prevailing rate.

In addition, The employee may also recover a reasonable attorney's fee, reasonable expert witness fees, and other costs of the action from the employer in addition to any judgment awarded by the court. However, if the employer's violation was made in good faith, and the employer had reasonable grounds for believing that no violation occurred, the court may reduce the employee's monetary award.

The employee may also obtain appropriate equitable relief, such as employment, reinstatement and promotion.

## FILING AN FMLA COMPLAINT WITH THE SECRETARY OF LABOR

An employee may file an FMLA complaint in person, by mail or by telephone, with the Wage and Hour Division, Employment Standards Administration, U.S. Department of Labor. In addition, a complaint may be filed at any local office of the Wage and Hour Division.

A directory of state department of labor offices is set forth at Appendix 5.

The complaint should be filed within a reasonable time after the employee discovers that his or her FMLA rights have been violated. In no event, however, may a complaint be filed more than two years after the alleged violation occurred, or three years in the case of a willful violation.

The complaint is not required to be in any particular form, however, it must be in writing and should include a full statement of the acts or omissions which constitute the alleged violation, including any relevant dates.

## VIOLATION OF THE POSTING REQUIREMENT

If an employer violates the posting requirement, as discussed in Chapter 8, and it is determined that the violation was willful, the Department of Labor may impose a civil money penalty. The Department of Labor will issue and serve a notice of penalty on the employer in person or by certified mail. Where service is not accepted, the notice may be served by regular mail.

## THE EMPLOYER'S RIGHT TO APPEAL

An employer is entitled to appeal the penalty by obtaining a review of the assessment from the Wage and Hour Regional Administrator for the region in which the alleged violation occurred. However, if the employer does not request a review, or fails to do so in a timely manner, the notice of the penalty constitutes the final ruling of the Secretary of Labor.

The petition for review is not required to be in any particular form, however, the petition must be in writing, and contain the legal and factual bases for the petition. The petition must be mailed to the Regional Administrator within 15 days of receipt of the notice of penalty. In addition, the employer may request an oral hearing that may be conducted by telephone. The Regional Administrator's decision on the petition constitutes the final order of the Secretary.

If the employer fails to pay the penalty assessment after the final order is issued, the Regional Administrator may seek to recover the unpaid penalty, including interest and additional penalties, by filing suit in court. The final order may also be referred to the Solicitor of Labor for collection.

## RETALIATION

The FMLA prohibits interference with an employee's rights under the law, and with legal proceedings or inquiries relating to an employee's rights, as set forth below.

### Interference With FMLA Rights

An employer is prohibited from interfering with, restraining, or denying the exercise of any rights provided by the FMLA. Any violations of the FMLA or its regulations constitute "interfering with, restraining, or denying" the exercise of rights provided by the FMLA.

Interfering with the exercise of an employee's rights would include, for example, not only refusing to authorize FMLA leave, but discouraging an employee from using such leave. Interference would also include manipulation by a covered employer to avoid responsibilities under the FMLA, such as:

1. Transferring employees from one worksite to another for the purpose of reducing worksites, or to keep worksites, below the 50-employee threshold for employee eligibility under the FMLA;

2. Changing the essential functions of the job in order to preclude the taking of leave;

3. Reducing hours available to work in order to avoid employee eligibility.

### Discrimination

An employer is prohibited from discharging or in any other way discriminating against any person for opposing or complaining about any unlawful practice under the FMLA. For example, if an employee on leave without pay would otherwise be entitled to full benefits—other than health benefits—the same benefits would be required to be provided to an employee on unpaid FMLA leave.

In addition, an employer is prohibited from discriminating against employees or prospective employees who have used FMLA leave, and cannot use the taking of FMLA leave as a negative factor in employment actions, such as hiring, promotion, or disciplinary action.

All persons are prohibited from discharging or in any other way discriminating against any person because that person has:

1. Filed any charge, or has instituted any proceeding under or related to the FMLA;

2. Given, or is about to give, any information in connection with an inquiry or proceeding relating to a right under the FMLA; and/or

3. Testified, or is about to testify, in any inquiry or proceeding relating to a right under the FMLA.

# CHAPTER 11:
# THE EFFECT OF THE FMLA ON OTHER FEDERAL, STATE AND LOCAL LAWS

## APPLICABILITY OF STATE FAMILY MEDICAL LEAVE LAWS

Eleven states, including California, Connecticut, Hawaii, Maine, Minnesota, New Jersey, Oregon, Rhode Island, Vermont, Washington and Wisconsin, and the District of Columbia, have enacted family medical leave laws similar to the Federal law. However, even though identical terminology may be used in both the Federal and state law, it does not always have an identical definition. For example, the term "serious health condition" may be used in both the Federal law and a state law, but defined differently by the statutory authority. The reader is advised, therefore, to examine the definition of the term as set forth in the language of the applicable statute and its regulations.

Covered employers must comply with the federal or state provision that provides the greater benefit to their employees. For example, a number of states have enacted family medical leave laws that provide greater amounts of leave and benefits than those provided by the FMLA. Nothing in the FMLA supersedes any provision of State or local law that provides greater family or medical leave rights than those provided by the FMLA. However, the Department of Labor does not enforce state family medical leave laws, and the states may not enforce the FMLA.

When an employee takes leave, he or she is not required to designate whether the leave they are taking is FMLA leave or leave under State law, and an employer must comply with the applicable provisions of both laws. However, an employer covered by one law and not the other only has to comply with the law under which the employer is covered. Similarly, an employee eligible under only one law can only receive benefits under that law.

A Federal/State Family Medical Leave Comparison Chart is set forth at Appendix 6.

### Leave Entitlement

If the employee's leave qualifies for FMLA leave and family medical leave under State law, the leave used counts against the employee's entitlement under both laws. For example:

1. If State law provides 16 weeks of leave entitlement over two years, an employee would be entitled to take 16 weeks one year under State law, and 12 weeks the next year under the FMLA. Health benefits maintenance under the FMLA would be applicable only to the first 12 weeks of leave entitlement each year. If the employee took 12 weeks the first year, the employee would be entitled to a maximum of 12 weeks the second year under the FMLA, not 16 weeks. An employee would not be entitled to 28 weeks in one year.

2. If State law provides half-pay for employees temporarily disabled because of pregnancy for six weeks, the employee would be entitled to an additional six weeks of unpaid FMLA leave, or accrued paid leave.

3. A shorter notice period under State law must be allowed by the employer unless an employer has already provided, or the employee is requesting, more leave than required under State law.

4. If State law provides for only one medical certification, no additional certifications may be required by the employer unless the employer has already provided, or the employee is requesting, more leave than required under State law.

5. If State law provides six weeks of leave, which may include leave to care for a seriously-ill grandparent or a "spouse equivalent," and leave was used for that purpose, the employee is still entitled to 12 weeks of FMLA leave, as the leave used was provided for a purpose not covered by the FMLA. However, if FMLA leave is used first for a purpose also provided under State law, and State leave has thereby been exhausted, the employer would not be required to provide additional leave to care for the grandparent or "spouse equivalent."

6. If State law prohibits mandatory leave beyond the actual period of pregnancy disability, an instructional employee of an educational agency subject to special FMLA rules may not be required to remain on leave until the end of the academic term, as permitted by the FMLA under certain circumstances.

## EMPLOYEE RIGHTS UNDER EMPLOYER PRACTICES AND COLLECTIVE BARGAINING AGREEMENTS

Nothing in the FMLA is intended to discourage employers from adopting or retaining more generous leave policies than those set forth in the FMLA. For example, if an employer, on its own, provides greater unpaid family leave rights than are afforded by the FMLA, the employer is not required to extend additional rights afforded by the FMLA, such as maintenance of health benefits, to the additional leave period not covered by the FMLA. Further, if an employee takes paid or unpaid leave and the employer does not designate the leave as FMLA leave, the leave taken does not count against an employee's FMLA entitlement.

Conversely, the rights established by the FMLA may not be diminished by any employment benefit program or collective bargaining plan. For example, a provision of a collective bargaining agreement that provides for reinstatement to a position that is not equivalent because of seniority is superseded by the FMLA.

## THE FMLA AND ANTI-DISCRIMINATION LAWS

Nothing in the FMLA modifies or affects any Federal or State law prohibiting discrimination on the basis of race, religion, color, national origin, sex, age, or disability, such as the Americans with Disabilities Act of 1990 (ADA), or Title VII of the Civil Rights Act of 1964. Thus, for example, the leave provisions of the FMLA are wholly distinct from the reasonable accommodation obligations of employers covered under the ADA, as discussed below.

The purpose of the FMLA is to make leave available to eligible employees and employers within its coverage, and not to limit already existing rights and protection. An employer must therefore provide leave under whichever statutory provision provides the greater rights to employees.

When an employer violates both the FMLA and an anti-discrimination law, an employee may be able to recover under either or both statutes, although double relief may not be awarded for the same loss.

## THE AMERICANS WITH DISABILITIES ACT OF 1990

If an employee is a qualified individual with a disability within the meaning of the ADA, the employer must make reasonable accommodations in accordance with the ADA. At the same time, the employer must afford an employee his or her FMLA rights. The employee's rights under both statutes must be analyzed separately. For example:

1. The FMLA entitles eligible employees to 12 weeks of leave in any 12-month period, whereas the ADA allows an indeterminate amount of leave, barring undue hardship, as a reasonable accommodation. In addition, the FMLA requires employers to maintain employees' group health plan coverage during FMLA leave on the same conditions as coverage would have been provided if the employee had been continuously employed during the leave period, whereas the ADA does not require maintenance of health insurance unless other employees receive health plan coverage.

2. A reasonable accommodation under the ADA might be accomplished by providing an individual with a disability with a part-time job with no health benefits, assuming the employer did not ordinarily provide health insurance for part-time employees. However, the FMLA would permit an employee to work a reduced leave schedule until the equivalent of 12 workweeks of leave were used, with group health benefits maintained during this period.

3. The FMLA permits an employer to temporarily transfer an employee who is taking leave intermittently or on a reduced leave schedule to an alternative position, whereas the ADA allows an accommodation of reassignment to an equivalent, vacant position only if the employee cannot perform the essential functions of the employee's present position and an accommodation is not possible in the employee's present position, or an accommodation in the employee's present position would cause an undue hardship for the employer.

## TITLE VII OF THE CIVIL RIGHTS ACT OF 1964

Under Title VII of the Civil Rights Act of 1964, as amended by the Pregnancy Discrimination Act, an employer should provide the same benefits for women who are pregnant as the employer provides to other employees with short-term disabilities. Because Title VII does not require employees to be employed for a certain period of time to be protected, an employee employed for less than 12 months by the employer—and therefore, not an "eligible" employee under FMLA—may not be denied maternity leave if the employer normally provides short-term disability benefits to employees who are experiencing other short-term disabilities.

# CHAPTER 12:
# SPECIAL FMLA RULES FOR MILITARY PERSONNEL

**THE UNIFORMED SERVICES EMPLOYMENT AND REEMPLOYMENT RIGHTS ACT (USERRA)**

The Uniformed Services Employment and Reemployment Rights Act (USERRA) is a Federal law enacted in 1994 that provides reemployment rights for veterans and members of the National Guard and Reserve following qualifying military service. It also prohibits employer discrimination against any person on the basis of that person's past military service, current military obligations or intent to join one of the uniformed services.

The USERRA entitles returning service members to all the benefits of employment that they would have obtained if they had been continuously employed. Thus, the USERRA requires that a person reemployed under its provisions be given credit for any months and hours of service he or she would have been employed but for their military service, in determining eligibility for FMLA leave.

**THE 12 MONTH/1,250 HOUR REQUIREMENT**

As set forth in Chapter 3, under ordinary circumstances, a worker becomes eligible for leave under the FMLA after working for a covered employer for at least 12 months, during which he or she completed at least 1,250 hours of work. However, a member of the National Guard or Reserve who is absent from employment for an extended period of time due to military service, and who requests FMLA leave shortly after returning to civilian employment, may not have actually worked for his or her employer for a total of 12 months, or may not have performed 1250 hours of actual work with the employer in the 12 months prior to the start of the FMLA leave.

Under the USERRA, the employer is required to count the months and hours that reservists or National Guards would have worked if they had not been called up for military service towards FMLA eligibility. That time must be combined with the months employed and the hours actually worked to meet the 12 months/1,250 hours FMLA requirement.

The service member's eligibility for FMLA leave will depend upon whether the service member would have met the eligibility requirements outlined above had he or she not performed military service.

### The 12-Month Requirement

If someone who has been employed by an employer for 9 months is ordered to active military service for 9 months, upon reemployment, the person must be considered to have been employed by the employer for more than the required 12 months—the 9 months actually employed plus the 9 months service in the military—for purposes of FMLA eligibility. It should be noted that the 12 months of employment do not have to be consecutive to meet this FMLA requirement.

### The 1,250 Hours of Service Requirement

An employee returning after military service should be credited with the hours of service that would have been performed but for the period of military service in determining FMLA eligibility. Accordingly, a person reemployed following military service has the hours that would have been worked for the employer added to any hours actually worked during the previous 12-month period to meet the 1,250 hour requirement.

In order to determine the hours that would have been worked during the period of military service, the employee's pre-service work schedule can generally be used for calculations. For example, an employee who works 40 hours per week for the employer returns to employment following 20 weeks of military service and requests leave under the FMLA. To determine the person's eligibility, the hours he or she would have worked during the period of military service (20 x 40 = 800 hours) must be added to the hours actually worked during the 12-month period prior to the start of the leave, to determine if the 1,250-hour requirement is met.

Additional information concerning the USERRA may be obtained by visiting the website for the Department of Labor's Veterans' Employment and Training at: http://www.dol.gov/vets/.

# APPENDIX 1:
# THE FAMILY AND MEDICAL LEAVE ACT OF 1993

1. SHORT TITLE; TABLE OF CONTENTS.
(a) SHORT TITLE.—This Act may be cited as the "Family and Medical Leave Act of 1993".
(b) TABLE OF CONTENTS

**TITLE V—COVERAGE OF CONGRESSIONAL EMPLOYEES**
SEC. 501. Leave for certain Senate employees.
SEC. 502. Leave for certain House employees.
**TITLE VI—SENSE OF CONGRESS**
SEC. 601. Sense of Congress.
### SEC. 2. FINDINGS AND PURPOSES.
(a) FINDINGS.—Congress finds that—

(1) the number of single-parent households and two-parent households in which the single parent or both parents work is increasing significantly;

(2) it is important for the development of children and the family unit that fathers and mothers be able to participate in early childrearing and the care of family members who have serious health conditions;

(3) the lack of employment policies to accommodate working parents can force individuals to choose between job security and parenting;

(4) there is inadequate job security for employees who have serious health conditions that prevent them from working for temporary periods;

(5) due to the nature of the roles of men and women in our society, the primary responsibility for family caretaking often falls on women, and such responsibility affects the working lives of women more than it affects the working lives of men; and

(6) employment standards that apply to one gender only have serious potential for encouraging employers to discriminate against employees and applicants for employment who are of that gender.

(b) PURPOSES.—It is the purpose of this Act—

(1) to balance the demands of the workplace with the needs of families, to promote the stability and economic security of families, and to promote national interests in preserving family integrity;

(2) to entitle employees to take reasonable leave for medical reasons, for the birth or adoption of a child, and for the care of a child, spouse, or parent who has a serious health condition;

(3) to accomplish the purposes described in paragraphs (1) and (2) in a manner that accommodates the legitimate interests of employers;

(4) to accomplish the purposes described in paragraphs (1) and (2) in a manner that, consistent with the Equal Protection Clause of the Fourteenth Amendment, minimizes the potential for employment discrimination on the basis of sex by ensuring generally that leave is available for eligible medical reasons (including maternity-related disability) and for compelling family reasons, on a gender-neutral basis; and

(5) to promote the goal of equal employment opportunity for women and men, pursuant to such clause.

## TITLE I—GENERAL REQUIREMENTS FOR LEAVE

**SEC. 101. DEFINITIONS.**

(1) COMMERCE.—The terms "commerce" and "industry or activity affecting commerce" mean any activity, business, or industry in commerce or in which a labor dispute would hinder or obstruct commerce or the free flow of commerce, and include "commerce" and any "industry affecting commerce", as defined in paragraphs (1) and (3) of section 501 of the Labor Management Relations Act, 1947 (29 U.S.C. 142 (1) and (3)).

(2) ELIGIBLE EMPLOYEE.—

(A) IN GENERAL.—The term "eligible employee" means an employee who has been employed

(i) for at least 12 months by the employer with respect to whom leave is requested under section 102; and

(ii) for at least 1,250 hours of service with such employer during the previous 12-month period.

(B) EXCLUSIONS.—The term "eligible employee" does not include

(i) any Federal officer or employee covered under subchapter V of chapter 63 of title 5, United States Code (as added by title II of this Act); or

(ii) any employee of an employer who is employed at a worksite at which such employer employs less than 50 employees if the total number of employees employed by that employer within 75 miles of that worksite is less than 50.

(C) DETERMINATION.—For purposes of determining whether an employee meets the hours of service requirement specified in subparagraph (A)(ii), the legal standards established under section 7 of the Fair Labor Standards Act of 1938 (29 U.S.C. 207) shall apply.

(3) EMPLOY; EMPLOYEE; STATE.—The terms "employ", "employee", and "State" have the same meanings given such terms in subsections (c), (e), and (g) of section 3 of the Fair Labor Standards Act of 1938 (29 U.S.C. 203(c), (e), and (g)).

(4) EMPLOYER.—

(A) IN GENERAL.—The term "employer"

(i) means any person engaged in commerce or in any industry or activity affecting commerce who employs 50 or more employees for each working day during each of 20 or more calendar workweeks in the current or preceding calendar year;

(ii) includes—

(I) any person who acts, directly or indirectly, in the interest of an employer to any of the employees of such employer; and

(II) any successor in interest of an employer; and

(iii) includes any "public agency", as defined in section 3(x) of the Fair Labor Standards Act of 1938 (29 U.S.C. 203(x)).

(B) PUBLIC AGENCY.—For purposes of subparagraph (A)(iii), a public agency shall be considered to be a person engaged in commerce or in an industry or activity affecting commerce.

(5) EMPLOYMENT BENEFITS.—The term "employment benefits" means all benefits provided or made available to employees by an employer, including group life insurance, health insurance, disability insurance, sick leave, annual leave, educational benefits, and pensions, regardless of whether such benefits are provided by a practice or written policy of an employer or through an "employee benefit plan", as defined in section 3(3) of the Employee Retirement Income Security Act of 1974 (29 U.S.C. 1002(3)).

(6) HEALTH CARE PROVIDER.—The term "health care provider" means—

(A) a doctor of medicine or osteopathy who is authorized to practice medicine or surgery (as appropriate) by the State in which the doctor practices; or

(B) any other person determined by the Secretary to be capable of providing health care services.

(7) PARENT.—The term "parent" means the biological parent of an employee or an individual who stood in loco parentis to an employee when the employee was a son or daughter.

(8) PERSON.—The term "person" has the same meaning given such term in section 3(a) of the Fair Labor Standards Act of 1938 (29 U.S.C. 203(a)).

(9) REDUCED LEAVE SCHEDULE.—The term "reduced leave schedule" means a leave schedule that reduces the usual number of hours per workweek, or hours per workday, of an employee.

(10) SECRETARY.—The term "Secretary" means the Secretary of Labor.

(11) SERIOUS HEALTH CONDITION. The term "serious health condition" means an illness, injury, impairment, or physical or mental condition that involves

(A) inpatient care in a hospital, hospice, or residential medical care facility; or

(B) continuing treatment by a health care provider.

(12) SON OR DAUGHTER.—The term "son or daughter" means a biological, adopted, or foster child, a stepchild, a legal ward, or a child of a person standing in loco parentis, who is—

(A) under 18 years of age; or

(B) 18 years of age or older and incapable of self-care because of a mental or physical disability.

(13) SPOUSE.—The term "spouse" means a husband or wife, as the case may be.

## SEC. 102. LEAVE REQUIREMENT.

(a) IN GENERAL.—

(1) ENTITLEMENT TO LEAVE.—Subject to section 103, an eligible employee shall be entitled to a total of 12 workweeks of leave during any 12-month period for one or more of the following:

(A) Because of the birth of a son or daughter of the employee and in order to care for such son or daughter.

(B) Because of the placement of a son or daughter with the employee for adoption or foster care.

(C) In order to care for the spouse, or a son, daughter, or parent, of the employee, if such spouse, son, daughter, or parent has a serious health condition.

(D) Because of a serious health condition that makes the employee unable to perform the functions of the position of such employee.

(2) EXPIRATION OF ENTITLEMENT.—The entitlement to leave under subparagraphs (A) and (B) of paragraph (1) for a birth or placement of a son or daughter shall expire at the end of the 12-month period beginning on the date of such birth or placement.

(b) LEAVE TAKEN INTERMITTENTLY OR ON A REDUCED LEAVE SCHEDULE.

(1) IN GENERAL.—Leave under subparagraph (A) or (B) of subsection (a)(1) shall not be taken by an employee intermittently or on a

reduced leave schedule unless the employee and the employer of the employee agree otherwise. Subject to paragraph (2), subsection (e)(2), and section 103(b)(5), leave under subparagraph (C) or (D) of subsection (a)(1) may be taken intermittently or on a reduced leave schedule when medically necessary. The taking of leave intermittently or on a reduced leave schedule pursuant to this paragraph shall not result in a reduction in the total amount of leave to which the employee is entitled under subsection (a) beyond the amount of leave actually taken.

(2) ALTERNATIVE POSITION.— If an employee requests intermittent leave, or leave on a reduced leave schedule, under subparagraph (C) or (D) of subsection (a)(1), that is foreseeable based on planned medical treatment, the employer may require such employee to transfer temporarily to an available alternative position offered by the employer for which the employee is qualified and that—

(A) has equivalent pay and benefits; and

(B) better accommodates recurring periods of leave than the regular employment position of the employee.

(c) UNPAID LEAVE PERMITTED.—Except as provided in subsection (d), leave granted under subsection (a) may consist of unpaid leave. Where an employee is otherwise exempt under regulations issued by the Secretary pursuant to section 13(a)(1) of the Fair Labor Standards Act of 1938 (29 U.S.C. 213(a)(1)), the compliance of an employer with this title by providing unpaid leave shall not affect the exempt status of the employee under such section.

(d) RELATIONSHIP TO PAID LEAVE.—

(1) UNPAID LEAVE.—If an employer provides paid leave for fewer than 12 workweeks, the additional weeks of leave necessary to attain the 12 workweeks of leave required under this title may be provided without compensation.

(2) SUBSTITUTION OF PAID LEAVE.—

(A) IN GENERAL.—An eligible employee may elect, or an employer may require the employee, to substitute any of the accrued paid vacation leave, personal leave, or family leave of the employee for leave provided under subparagraph (A), (B), or (C) of subsection (a)(1) for any part of the 12-week period of such leave under such subsection.

(B) SERIOUS HEALTH CONDITION.—An eligible employee may elect, or an employer may require the employee, to substitute any of the accrued paid vacation leave, personal leave, or medical or sick leave of the employee for leave provided under subparagraph (C) or (D) of subsection (a)(1) for any part of the 12-week period of such leave under such subsection, except that nothing in this title shall require an employer to provide paid sick leave or paid medical leave in any situation in which such employer would not normally provide any such paid leave.

(e) FORESEEABLE LEAVE.—

(1) REQUIREMENT OF NOTICE.—In any case in which the necessity for leave under subparagraph (A) or (B) of subsection (a)(1) is foreseeable based on an expected birth or placement, the employee shall provide the employer with not less than 30 days' notice, before the date the leave is to begin, of the employee's intention to take leave under such subparagraph, except that if the date of the birth or placement requires leave to begin in less than 30 days, the employee shall provide such notice as is practicable.

(2) DUTIES OF EMPLOYEE.—In any case in which the necessity for leave under subparagraph (C) or (D) of subsection (a)(1) is foreseeable based on planned medical treatment, the employee—

(A) shall make a reasonable effort to schedule the treatment so as not to disrupt unduly the operations of the employer, subject to the approval of the health care provider of the employee or the health care provider of the son, daughter, spouse, or parent of the employee, as appropriate; and

(B) shall provide the employer with not less than 30 days' notice, before the date the leave is to begin, of the employee's intention to take leave under such subparagraph, except that if the date of the treatment requires leave to begin in less than 30 days, the employee shall provide such notice as is practicable.

(f) SPOUSES EMPLOYED BY THE SAME EMPLOYER.—In any case in which a husband and wife entitled to leave under subsection (a) are employed by the same employer, the aggregate number of workweeks of leave to which both may be entitled may be limited to 12 workweeks during any 12-month period, if such leave is taken—

(1) under subparagraph (A) or (B) of subsection (a)(1); or

(2) to care for a sick parent under subparagraph (C) of such subsection.

## SEC. 103. CERTIFICATION.

(a) IN GENERAL.—An employer may require that a request for leave under subparagraph (C) or (D) of section 102(a)(1) be supported by a certification issued by the health care provider of the eligible employee or of the son, daughter, spouse, or parent of the employee, as appropriate. The employee shall provide, in a timely manner, a copy of such certification to the employer.

(b) SUFFICIENT CERTIFICATION.—Certification provided under subsection (a) shall be sufficient if it states

(1) the date on which the serious health condition commenced;

(2) the probable duration of the condition;

(3) the appropriate medical facts within the knowledge of the health care provider regarding the condition;

(4)(A) for purposes of leave under section 102(a)(1)(C), a statement that the eligible employee is needed to care for the son, daughter, spouse, or parent and an estimate of the amount of time that such employee is needed to care for the son, daughter, spouse, or parent; and

(4)(B) for purposes of leave under section 102(a)(1)(D), a statement that the employee is unable to perform the functions of the position of the employee;

(5) in the case of certification for intermittent leave, or leave on a reduced leave schedule, for planned medical treatment, the dates on which such treatment is expected to be given and the duration of such treatment;

(6) in the case of certification for intermittent leave, or leave on a reduced leave schedule, under section 102(a)(1)(D), a statement of the medical necessity for the intermittent leave or leave on a reduced leave schedule, and the expected duration of the intermittent leave or reduced leave schedule; and

(7) in the case of certification for intermittent leave, or leave on a reduced leave schedule, under section 102(a)(1)(C), a statement that the employee's intermittent leave or leave on a reduced leave schedule is necessary for the care of the son, daughter, parent, or spouse who has a serious health condition, or will assist in their recovery, and the expected duration and schedule of the intermittent leave or reduced leave schedule.

(c) SECOND OPINION.—

(1) IN GENERAL.—In any case in which the employer has reason to doubt the validity of the certification provided under subsection (a) for leave under subparagraph (C) or (D) of section 102(a)(1), the employer may require, at the expense of the employer, that the eligible employee obtain the opinion of a second health care provider desig-

nated or approved by the employer concerning any information certified under subsection (b) for such leave.

(2) LIMITATION.—A health care provider designated or approved under paragraph (1) shall not be employed on a regular basis by the employer.

(d) RESOLUTION OF CONFLICTING OPINIONS.—

(1) IN GENERAL.—In any case in which the second opinion described in subsection (c) differs from the opinion in the original certification provided under subsection (a), the employer may require, at the expense of the employer, that the employee obtain the opinion of a third health care provider designated or approved jointly by the employer and the employee concerning the information certified under subsection (b).

(2) FINALITY.—The opinion of the third health care provider concerning the information certified under subsection (b) shall be considered to be final and shall be binding on the employer and the employee.

(e) SUBSEQUENT RECERTIFICATION.—The employer may require that the eligible employee obtain subsequent recertifications on a reasonable basis.

## SEC. 104. EMPLOYMENT AND BENEFITS PROTECTION.

(a) RESTORATION TO POSITION.—

(1) IN GENERAL.—Except as provided in subsection (b), any eligible employee who takes leave under section 102 for the intended purpose of the leave shall be entitled, on return from such leave—

(A) to be restored by the employer to the position of employment held by the employee when the leave commenced; or

(B) to be restored to an equivalent position with equivalent employment benefits, pay, and other terms and conditions of employment.

(2) LOSS OF BENEFITS.—The taking of leave under section 102 shall not result in the loss of any employment benefit accrued prior to the date on which the leave commenced.

(3) LIMITATIONS.—Nothing in this section shall be construed to entitle any restored employee to—

(A) the accrual of any seniority or employment benefits during any period of leave; or

(B) any right, benefit, or position of employment other than any right, benefit, or position to which the employee would have been entitled had the employee not taken the leave.

(4) CERTIFICATION.—As a condition of restoration under paragraph (1) for an employee who has taken leave under section 102(a)(1)(D), the employer may have a uniformly applied practice or policy that requires each such employee to receive certification from the health care provider of the employee that the employee is able to resume work, except that nothing in this paragraph shall supersede a valid State or local law or a collective bargaining agreement that governs the return to work of such employees.

(5) CONSTRUCTION.—Nothing in this subsection shall be construed to prohibit an employer from requiring an employee on leave under section 102 to report periodically to the employer on the status and intention of the employee to return to work.

(b) EXEMPTION CONCERNING CERTAIN HIGHLY COMPENSATED EMPLOYEES.—

(1) DENIAL OF RESTORATION.—An employer may deny restoration under subsection (a) to any eligible employee described in paragraph (2) if—

(A) such denial is necessary to prevent substantial and grievous economic injury to the operations of the employer;

(B) the employer notifies the employee of the intent of the employer to deny restoration on such basis at the time the employer determines that such injury would occur; and

(C) in any case in which the leave has commenced, the employee elects not to return to employment after receiving such notice.

(2) AFFECTED EMPLOYEES.—An eligible employee described in paragraph (1) is a salaried eligible employee who is among the highest paid 10 percent of the employees employed by the employer within 75 miles of the facility at which the employee is employed.

(c) MAINTENANCE OF HEALTH BENEFITS.—

(1) COVERAGE.—Except as provided in paragraph (2), during any period that an eligible employee takes leave under section 102, the employer shall maintain coverage under any "group health plan" (as defined in section 5000(b)(1) of the Internal Revenue Code of 1986) for the duration of such leave at the level and under the conditions coverage would have been provided if the employee had continued in employment continuously for the duration of such leave.

(2) FAILURE TO RETURN FROM LEAVE.—The employer may recover the premium that the employer paid for maintaining coverage for the employee under such group health plan during any period of unpaid leave under section 102 if—

(A) the employee fails to return from leave under section 102 after the period of leave to which the employee is entitled has expired; and

(B) the employee fails to return to work for a reason other than—

(i) the continuation, recurrence, or onset of a serious health condition that entitles the employee to leave under subparagraph (C) or (D) of section 102(a)(1); or

(ii) other circumstances beyond the control of the employee.

(3) CERTIFICATION.—

(A) ISSUANCE.—An employer may require that a claim that an employee is unable to return to work because of the continuation, recurrence, or onset of the serious health condition described in paragraph (2)(B)(i) be supported by—

(i) a certification issued by the health care provider of the son, daughter, spouse, or parent of the employee, as appropriate, in the case of an employee unable to return to work because of a condition specified in section 102(a)(1)(C); or

(ii) a certification issued by the health care provider of the eligible employee, in the case of an employee unable to return to work because of a condition specified in section 102(a)(1)(D).

(B) COPY.—The employee shall provide, in a timely manner, a copy of such certification to the employer.

(C) SUFFICIENCY OF CERTIFICATION.—

(i) LEAVE DUE TO SERIOUS HEALTH CONDITION OF EMPLOYEE.—The certification described in subparagraph (A)(ii) shall be sufficient if the certification states that a serious health condition prevented the employee from being able to perform the functions of the position of the employee on the date that the leave of the employee expired.

(ii) LEAVE DUE TO SERIOUS HEALTH CONDITION OF FAMILY MEMBER.—The certification described in subparagraph (A)(i) shall be sufficient if the certification states that the employee is needed to care for the son, daughter, spouse, or parent who has a serious health condition on the date that the leave of the employee expired.

### SEC. 105. PROHIBITED ACTS.

(a) INTERFERENCE WITH RIGHTS.—

(1) EXERCISE OF RIGHTS.—It shall be unlawful for any employer to interfere with, restrain, or deny the exercise of or the attempt to exercise, any right provided under this title.

(2) DISCRIMINATION.—It shall be unlawful for any employer to discharge or in any other manner discriminate against any individual for opposing any practice made unlawful by this title.

(b) INTERFERENCE WITH PROCEEDINGS OR INQUIRIES.—It shall be unlawful for any person to discharge or in any other manner discriminate against any individual because such individual—

(1) has filed any charge, or has instituted or caused to be instituted any proceeding, under or related to this title;

(2) has given, or is about to give, any information in connection with any inquiry or proceeding relating to any right provided under this title; or

(3) has testified, or is about to testify, in any inquiry or proceeding relating to any right provided under this title.

### SEC. 106. INVESTIGATIVE AUTHORITY.

(a) IN GENERAL.—To ensure compliance with the provisions of this title, or any regulation or order issued under this title, the Secretary shall have, subject to subsection (c), the investigative authority provided under section 11(a) of the Fair Labor Standards Act of 1938 (29 U.S.C. 211(a)).

(b) OBLIGATION TO KEEP AND PRESERVE RECORDS.—Any employer shall make, keep, and preserve records pertaining to compliance with this title in accordance with section 11(c) of the Fair Labor Standards Act of 1938 (29 U.S.C. 211(c)) and in accordance with regulations issued by the Secretary.

(c) REQUIRED SUBMISSIONS GENERALLY LIMITED TO AN ANNUAL BASIS.—The Secretary shall not under the authority of this section require any employer or any plan, fund, or program to submit to the Secretary any books or records more than once during any 12-month period, unless the Secretary has reasonable cause to believe there may exist a violation of this title or any regulation or order issued pursuant to this title, or is investigating a charge pursuant to section 107(b).

(d) SUBPOENA POWERS.—For the purposes of any investigation provided for in this section, the Secretary shall have the subpoena authority provided for under section 9 of the Fair Labor Standards Act of 1938 (29 U.S.C. 209).

## SEC. 107. ENFORCEMENT.

(a) CIVIL ACTION BY EMPLOYEES.—

(1) LIABILITY.—Any employer who violates section 105 shall be liable to any eligible employee affected—

(A) for damages equal to—

(i) the amount of—

(I) any wages, salary, employment benefits, or other compensation denied or lost to such employee by reason of the violation; or

(II) in a case in which wages, salary, employment benefits, or other compensation have not been denied or lost to the employee, any actual monetary losses sustained by the employee as a direct result of the violation, such as the cost of providing care, up to a sum equal to 12 weeks of wages or salary for the employee;

(ii) the interest on the amount described in clause (i) calculated at the prevailing rate; and

(iii) an additional amount as liquidated damages equal to the sum of the amount described in clause (i) and the interest described in clause (ii), except that if an employer who has violated section 105 proves to the satisfaction of the court that the act or omission which violated section 105 was in good faith and that the employer had reasonable grounds for believing that the act or omission was not a violation of section 105, such court may, in the discretion of the court, reduce the amount of the liability to the amount and interest determined under clauses (i) and (ii), respectively; and

(B) for such equitable relief as may be appropriate, including employment, reinstatement, and promotion.

(2) RIGHT OF ACTION.—An action to recover the damages or equitable relief prescribed in paragraph (1) may be maintained against any employer (including a public agency) in any Federal or State court of competent jurisdiction by any one or more employees for and in behalf of—

(A) the employees; or

(B) the employees and other employees similarly situated.

(3) FEES AND COSTS.—The court in such an action shall, in addition to any judgment awarded to the plaintiff, allow a reasonable attorney's fee, reasonable expert witness fees, and other costs of the action to be paid by the defendant.

(4) LIMITATIONS.—The right provided by paragraph (2) to bring an action by or on behalf of any employee shall terminate—

(A) on the filing of a complaint by the Secretary in an action under subsection (d) in which restraint is sought of any further delay in the payment of the amount described in paragraph (1)(A) to such employee by an employer responsible under paragraph (1) for the payment; or

(B) on the filing of a complaint by the Secretary in an action under subsection (b) in which a recovery is sought of the damages described in paragraph (1)(A) owing to an eligible employee by an employer liable under paragraph (1), unless the action described in subparagraph (A) or (B) is dismissed without prejudice on motion of the Secretary.

(b) ACTION BY THE SECRETARY.—

(1) ADMINISTRATIVE ACTION.—The Secretary shall receive, investigate, and attempt to resolve complaints of violations of section 105 in the same manner that the Secretary receives, investigates, and attempts to resolve complaints of violations of sections 6 and 7 of the Fair Labor Standards Act of 1938 (29 U.S.C. 206 and 207).

(2) CIVIL ACTION.—The Secretary may bring an action in any court of competent jurisdiction to recover the damages described in subsection (a)(1)(A).

(3) SUMS RECOVERED.—Any sums recovered by the Secretary pursuant to paragraph (2) shall be held in a special deposit account and shall be paid, on order of the Secretary, directly to each employee affected. Any such sums not paid to an employee because of inability to do so within a period of 3 years shall be deposited into the Treasury of the United States as miscellaneous receipts.

(c) LIMITATION.—

(1) IN GENERAL.—Except as provided in paragraph (2), an action may be brought under this section not later than 2 years after the date of the last event constituting the alleged violation for which the action is brought.

(2) WILLFUL VIOLATION.—In the case of such action brought for a willful violation of section 105, such action may be brought within 3

years of the date of the last event constituting the alleged violation for which such action is brought.

(3) COMMENCEMENT.—In determining when an action is commenced by the Secretary under this section for the purposes of this subsection, it shall be considered to be commenced on the date when the complaint is filed.

(d) ACTION FOR INJUNCTION BY SECRETARY.—The district courts of the United States shall have jurisdiction, for cause shown, in an action brought by the Secretary—

(1) to restrain violations of section 105, including the restraint of any withholding of payment of wages, salary, employment benefits, or other compensation, plus interest, found by the court to be due to eligible employees; or

(2) to award such other equitable relief as may be appropriate, including employment, reinstatement, and promotion.

(e) SOLICITOR OF LABOR.—The Solicitor of Labor may appear for and represent the Secretary on any litigation brought under this section.

## SEC. 108. SPECIAL RULES CONCERNING EMPLOYEES OF LOCAL EDUCATIONAL AGENCIES.

(a) APPLICATION.—

(1) IN GENERAL.—Except as otherwise provided in this section, the rights (including the rights under section 104, which shall extend throughout the period of leave of any employee under this section), remedies, and procedures under this title shall apply to—

(A) any "local educational agency" (as defined in section 1471(12) of the Elementary and Secondary Education Act of 1965 (20 U.S.C. 2891(12))) and an eligible employee of the agency; and

(B) any private elementary or secondary school and an eligible employee of the school.

(2) DEFINITIONS.—For purposes of the application described in paragraph (1):

(A) ELIGIBLE EMPLOYEE.—The term "eligible employee" means an eligible employee of an agency or school described in paragraph (1).

(B) EMPLOYER.—The term "employer" means an agency or school described in paragraph (1).

(b) LEAVE DOES NOT VIOLATE CERTAIN OTHER FEDERAL LAWS.— A local educational agency and a private elementary or secondary school shall not be in violation of the Individuals with Disabilities Education Act (20 U.S.C. 1400 et seq.), section 504 of the Rehabilitation Act of 1973 (29 U.S.C. 794), or title VI of the Civil Rights Act of 1964 (42 U.S.C. 2000d et seq.), solely as a result of an eligible employee of such agency or school exercising the rights of such employee under this title.

(c) INTERMITTENT LEAVE OR LEAVE ON A REDUCED SCHEDULE FOR INSTRUCTIONAL EMPLOYEES.—

(1) IN GENERAL.—Subject to paragraph (2), in any case in which an eligible employee employed principally in an instructional capacity by any such educational agency or school requests leave under subparagraph (C) or (D) of section 102(a)(1) that is foreseeable based on planned medical treatment and the employee would be on leave for greater than 20 percent of the total number of working days in the period during which the leave would extend, the agency or school may require that such employee elect either—

(A) to take leave for periods of a particular duration, not to exceed the duration of the planned medical treatment; or

(B) to transfer temporarily to an available alternative position offered by the employer for which the employee is qualified, and that—

(i) has equivalent pay and benefits; and

(ii) better accommodates recurring periods of leave than the regular employment position of the employee.

(2) APPLICATION.—The elections described in subparagraphs (A) and (B) of paragraph (1) shall apply only with respect to an eligible employee who complies with section 102(e)(2).

(d) RULES APPLICABLE TO PERIODS NEAR THE CONCLUSION OF AN ACADEMIC TERM.—The following rules shall apply with respect to periods of leave near the conclusion of an academic term in the case of any eligible employee employed principally in an instructional capacity by any such educational agency or school:

(1) LEAVE MORE THAN 5 WEEKS PRIOR TO END OF TERM.—If the eligible employee begins leave under section 102 more than 5 weeks prior to the end of the academic term, the agency or school may require the employee to continue taking leave until the end of such term, if—

(A) the leave is of at least 3 weeks duration; and

(B) the return to employment would occur during the 3-week period before the end of such term.

(2) LEAVE LESS THAN 5 WEEKS PRIOR TO END OF TERM.—If the eligible employee begins leave under subparagraph (A), (B), or (C) of section 102(a)(1) during the period that commences 5 weeks prior to the end of the academic term, the agency or school may require the employee to continue taking leave until the end of such term, if—

(A) the leave is of greater than 2 weeks duration; and

(B) the return to employment would occur during the 2-week period before the end of such term.

(3) LEAVE LESS THAN 3 WEEKS PRIOR TO END OF TERM.—If the eligible employee begins leave under subparagraph (A), (B), or (C) of section 102(a)(1) during the period that commences 3 weeks prior to the end of the academic term and the duration of the leave is greater than 5 working days, the agency or school may require the employee to continue to take leave until the end of such term.

(e) RESTORATION TO EQUIVALENT EMPLOYMENT POSITION.—For purposes of determinations under section 104(a)(1)(B) (relating to the restoration of an eligible employee to an equivalent position), in the case of a local educational agency or a private elementary or secondary school, such determination shall be made on the basis of established school board policies and practices, private school policies and practices, and collective bargaining agreements.

(f) REDUCTION OF THE AMOUNT OF LIABILITY.—If a local educational agency or a private elementary or secondary school that has violated this title proves to the satisfaction of the court that the agency, school, or department had reasonable grounds for believing that the underlying act or omission was not a violation of this title, such court may, in the discretion of the court, reduce the amount of the liability provided for under section 107(a)(1)(A) to the amount and interest determined under clauses (i) and (ii), respectively, of such section.

## SEC. 109. NOTICE.

(a) IN GENERAL.—Each employer shall post and keep posted, in conspicuous places on the premises of the employer where notices to employees and applicants for employment are customarily posted, a notice, to be prepared or approved by the Secretary, setting forth excerpts from, or summaries of, the pertinent provisions of this title and information pertaining to the filing of a charge.

(b) PENALTY.—Any employer that willfully violates this section may be assessed a civil money penalty not to exceed $100 for each separate offense.

## TITLE II—LEAVE FOR CIVIL SERVICE EMPLOYEES

### SEC. 201. LEAVE REQUIREMENT.

(a) CIVIL SERVICE EMPLOYEES.—

(1) IN GENERAL.—Chapter 63 of title 5, United States Code, is amended by adding at the end the following new subchapter:

### "SUBCHAPTER V—FAMILY AND MEDICAL LEAVE

#### 6381. Definitions

"For the purpose of this subchapter—

"(1) the term 'employee' means any individual who—

"(A) is an 'employee', as defined by section 6301(2), including any individual employed in a position referred to in clause (v) or (ix) of section 6301(2), but excluding any individual employed by the government of the District of Columbia and any individual employed on a temporary or intermittent basis; and

"(B) has completed at least 12 months of service as an employee (within the meaning of subparagraph (A));

"(2) the term 'health care provider' means—

"(A) a doctor of medicine or osteopathy who is authorized to practice medicine or surgery (as appropriate) by the State in which the doctor practices; and

"(B) any other person determined by the Director of the Office of Personnel Management to be capable of providing health care services;

"(3) the term 'parent' means the biological parent of an employee or an individual who stood in loco parentis to an employee when the employee was a son or daughter;

"(4) the term 'reduced leave schedule' means a leave schedule that reduces the usual number of hours per workweek, or hours per workday, of an employee;

"(5) the term 'serious health condition' means an illness, injury, impairment, or physical or mental condition that involves—

"(A) inpatient care in a hospital, hospice, or residential medical care facility; or

"(B) continuing treatment by a health care provider; and

"(6) the term 'son or daughter' means a biological, adopted, or foster child, a stepchild, a legal ward, or a child of a person standing in loco parentis, who is—

"(A) under 18 years of age; or

"(B) 18 years of age or older and incapable of self-care because of a mental or physical disability.

## "6382. Leave requirement

"(a)(1) Subject to section 6383, an employee shall be entitled to a total of 12 administrative workweeks of leave during any 12-month period for one or more of the following:

"(A) Because of the birth of a son or daughter of the employee and in order to care for such son or daughter.

"(B) Because of the placement of a son or daughter with the employee for adoption or foster care.

"(C) In order to care for the spouse, or a son, daughter, or parent, of the employee, if such spouse, son, daughter, or parent has a serious health condition.

"(D) Because of a serious health condition that makes the employee unable to perform the functions of the employee's position.

"(2) The entitlement to leave under subparagraph (A) or (B) of paragraph (1) based on the birth or placement of a son or daughter shall expire at the end of the 12-month period beginning on the date of such birth or placement.

"(b)(1) Leave under subparagraph (A) or (B) of subsection (a)(1) shall not be taken by an employee intermittently or on a reduced leave schedule unless the employee and the employing agency of the employee agree otherwise. Subject to paragraph (2), subsection (e)(2), and section 6383(b)(5), leave under subparagraph (C) or (D) of subsection (a)(1) may be taken intermittently or on a reduced leave schedule when medically necessary. In the case of an employee who takes leave intermittently or on a reduced leave schedule pursuant to this paragraph, any hours of leave so taken by such employee shall be subtracted from the total amount of leave remaining available to such employee under subsection (a), for purposes of the 12-month period involved, on an hour-for-hour basis.

"(2) If an employee requests intermittent leave, or leave on a reduced leave schedule, under subparagraph (C) or (D) of subsection (a)(1); that is foreseeable based on planned medical treatment, the employing agency may require such employee to transfer temporarily to an available alternative position offered by the employing agency for which the employee is qualified and that—

"(A) has equivalent pay and benefits; and

"(B) better accommodates recurring periods of leave than the regular employment position of the employee.

"(c) Except as provided in subsection (d), leave granted under subsection (a) shall be leave without pay.

"(d) An employee may elect to substitute for leave under subparagraph (A), (B), (C), or (D) of subsection (a)(1) any of the employee's accrued or accumulated annual or sick leave under subchapter I for any part of the 12-week period of leave under such subsection, except that nothing in this subchapter shall require an employing agency to provide paid sick leave in any situation in which such employing agency would not normally provide any such paid leave.

"(e)(1) In any case in which the necessity for leave under subparagraph (A) or (B) of subsection (a)(1) is foreseeable based on an expected birth or placement, the employee shall provide the employing agency with not less than 30 days' notice, before the date the leave is to begin, of the employee's intention to take leave under such subparagraph, except that if the date of the birth or placement requires leave to begin in less than 30 days, the employee shall provide such notice as is practicable.

"(2) In any case in which the necessity for leave under subparagraph (C) or (D) of subsection (a)(1) is foreseeable based on planned medical treatment, the employee—

"(A) shall make a reasonable effort to schedule the treatment so as not to disrupt unduly the operations of the employing agency, subject to the approval of the health care provider of the employee or the health care provider of the son, daughter, spouse, or parent of the employee, as appropriate; and

"(B) shall provide the employing agency with not less than 30 days' notice, before the date the leave is to begin, of the employee's intention to take leave under such subparagraph, except that if the date of the treatment requires leave to begin in less than 30 days, the employee shall provide such notice as is practicable.

## "6383. Certification

"(a) An employing agency may require that a request for leave under subparagraph (C) or (D) of section 6382(a)(1) be supported by certification issued by the health care provider of the employee or of the son, daughter, spouse, or parent of the employee, as appropriate. The employee shall provide, in a timely manner, a copy of such certification to the employing agency.

"(b) A certification provided under subsection (a) shall be sufficient if it states—

"(1) the date on which the serious health condition commenced;

"(2) the probable duration of the condition;

"(3) the appropriate medical facts within the knowledge of the health care provider regarding the condition;

"(4)(A) for purposes of leave under section 6382(a)(1)(C), a statement that the employee is needed to care for the son, daughter, spouse, or parent, and an estimate of the amount of time that such employee is needed to care for such son, daughter, spouse, or parent; and

"(B) for purposes of leave under section 6382(a)(1)(D), a statement that the employee is unable to perform the functions of the position of the employee; and

"(5) in the case of certification for intermittent leave, or leave on a reduced leave schedule, for planned medical treatment, the dates on which such treatment is expected to be given and the duration of such treatment.

"(c)(1) In any case in which the employing agency has reason to doubt the validity of the certification provided under subsection (a) for leave under subparagraph (C) or (D) of section 6382(a)(1), the employing agency may require, at the expense of the agency, that the employee obtain the opinion of a second health care provider designated or approved by the employing agency concerning any information certified under subsection (b) for such leave.

"(2) Any health care provider designated or approved under paragraph (1) shall not be employed on a regular basis by the employing agency.

"(d)(1) In any case in which the second opinion described in subsection (c) differs from the original certification provided under subsection (a), the employing agency may require, at the expense of the agency, that the employee obtain the opinion of a third health care provider designated or approved jointly by the employing agency and the employee concerning the information certified under subsection (b).

"(2) The opinion of the third health care provider concerning the information certified under subsection (b) shall be considered to be final and shall be binding on the employing agency and the employee.

"(e) The employing agency may require, at the expense of the agency, that the employee obtain subsequent recertifications on a reasonable basis.

### "6384. Employment and benefits protection

"(a) Any employee who takes leave under section 6382 for the intended purpose of the leave shall be entitled, upon return from such leave—

"(1) to be restored by the employing agency to the position held by the employee when the leave commenced; or

"(2) to be restored to an equivalent position with equivalent benefits, pay, status, and other terms and conditions of employment.

"(b) The taking of leave under section 6382 shall not result in the loss of any employment benefit accrued prior to the date on which the leave commenced.

"(c) Except as otherwise provided by or under law, nothing in this section shall be construed to entitle any restored employee to—

"(1) the accrual of any employment benefits during any period of leave; or

"(2) any right, benefit, or position of employment other than any right, benefit, or position to which the employee would have been entitled had the employee not taken the leave.

"(d) As a condition to restoration under subsection (a) for an employee who takes leave under section 6382(a)(1)(D), the employing agency may have a uniformly applied practice or policy that requires each such employee to receive certification from the health care provider of the employee that the employee is able to resume work.

"(e) Nothing in this section shall be construed to prohibit an employing agency from requiring an employee on leave under section 6382 to report periodically to the employing agency on the status and intention of the employee to return to work.

### "6385. Prohibition of coercion

"(a) An employee shall not directly or indirectly intimidate, threaten, or coerce, or attempt to intimidate, threaten, or coerce, any other employee for the purpose of interfering with the exercise of any rights which such other employee may have under this subchapter.

"(b) For the purpose of this section—

"(1) the term "intimidate, threaten, or coerce' includes promising to confer or conferring any benefit (such as appointment, promotion, or compensation), or taking or threatening to take any reprisal (such as deprivation of appointment, promotion, or compensation); and

"(2) the term 'employee' means any 'employee', as defined by section 2105.

### "6386. Health insurance

"An employee enrolled in a health benefits plan under chapter 89 who is placed in a leave status under section 6382 may elect to continue the health benefits enrollment of the employee while in such leave status and arrange to pay currently into the Employees Health Benefits Fund (described in section 8909), the appropriate employee contributions.

### "6387. Regulations

"The Office of Personnel Management shall prescribe regulations necessary for the administration of this subchapter. The regulations prescribed under this subchapter shall, to the extent appropriate, be consistent with the regulations prescribed by the Secretary of Labor to carry out title I of the Family and Medical Leave Act of 1993.".

(2) TABLE OF CONTENTS.—The table of contents for chapter 63 of title 5, United States Code, is amended by adding at the end the following:

### "SUBCHAPTER V—FAMILY AND MEDICAL LEAVE

"6381. Definitions.

"6382. Leave requirement.

"6383. Certification.

"6384. Employment and benefits protection.

"6385. Prohibition of coercion.

"6386. Health insurance.

"6387. Regulations.".

(b) EMPLOYEES PAID FROM NONAPPROPRIATED FUNDS.—Section 2105(c)(1) of title 5, United States Code, is amended—

(1) by striking "or" at the end of subparagraph (C); and

(2) by adding at the end the following new subparagraph:

"(E) subchapter V of chapter 63, which shall be applied so as to construe references to benefit programs to refer to applicable programs for employees paid from nonappropriated funds; or".

## TITLE III—COMMISSION ON LEAVE

### SEC. 301. ESTABLISHMENT.

There is established a commission to be known as the Commission on Leave (referred to in this title as the "Commission").

### SEC. 302. DUTIES.

The Commission shall—

(1) conduct a comprehensive study of—

(A) existing and proposed mandatory and voluntary policies relating to family and temporary medical leave, including policies provided by employers not covered under this Act;

(B) the potential costs, benefits, and impact on productivity, job creation and business growth of such policies on employers and employees;

(C) possible differences in costs, benefits, and impact on productivity, job creation and business growth of such policies on employers based on business type and size;

(D) the impact of family and medical leave policies on the availability of employee benefits provided by employers, including employers not covered under this Act;

(E) alternate and equivalent State enforcement of title I with respect to employees described in section 108(a);

(F) methods used by employers to reduce administrative costs of implementing family and medical leave policies;

(G) the ability of the employers to recover, under section 104(c)(2), the premiums described in such section; and

(H) the impact on employers and employees of policies that provide temporary wage replacement during periods of family and medical leave.

(2) not later than 2 years after the date on which the Commission first meets, prepare and submit, to the appropriate Committees of Congress, a report concerning the subjects listed in paragraph (1).

## SEC. 303. MEMBERSHIP.

(a) COMPOSITION.—

(1) APPOINTMENTS.—The Commission shall be composed of 12 voting members and 4 ex officio members to be appointed not later than 60 days after the date of the enactment of this Act as follows:

(A) SENATORS.—One Senator shall be appointed by the Majority Leader of the Senate, and one Senator shall be appointed by the Minority Leader of the Senate.

(B) MEMBERS OF HOUSE OF REPRESENTATIVES.—One Member of the House of Representatives shall be appointed by the Speaker of the House of Representatives, and one Member of the House of Representatives shall be appointed by the Minority Leader of the House of Representatives.

(C) ADDITIONAL MEMBERS.—

(i) APPOINTMENT.—Two members each shall be appointed by

(I) the Speaker of the House of Representatives;

(II) the Majority Leader of the Senate;

(III) the Minority Leader of the House of Representatives; and

(IV) the Minority Leader of the Senate.

(ii) EXPERTISE.—Such members shall be appointed by virtue of demonstrated expertise in relevant family, temporary disability, and labor management issues. Such members shall include representatives of employers, including employers from large businesses and from small businesses.

(2) EX OFFICIO MEMBERS.—The Secretary of Health and Human Services, the Secretary of Labor, the Secretary of Commerce, and the Administrator of the Small Business Administration shall serve on the Commission as nonvoting ex officio members.

(b) VACANCIES.—Any vacancy on the Commission shall be filled in the manner in which the original appointment was made. The vacancy shall not affect the power of the remaining members to execute the duties of the Commission.

(c) CHAIRPERSON AND VICE CHAIRPERSON.—The Commission shall elect a chairperson and a vice chairperson from among the members of the Commission.

(d) QUORUM.—Eight members of the Commission shall constitute a quorum for all purposes, except that a lesser number may constitute a quorum for the purpose of holding hearings.

### SEC. 304. COMPENSATION.

(a) PAY.—Members of the Commission shall serve without compensation.

(b) TRAVEL EXPENSES.—Members of the Commission shall be allowed reasonable travel expenses, including a per diem allowance, in accordance with section 5703 of title 5, United States Code, when performing duties of the Commission.

### SEC. 305. POWERS.

(a) MEETINGS.—The Commission shall first meet not later than 30 days after the date on which all members are appointed, and the Commission shall meet thereafter on the call of the chairperson or a majority of the members.

(b) HEARINGS AND SESSIONS.—The Commission may hold such hearings, sit and act at such times and places, take such testimony, and receive such evidence as the Commission considers appropriate. The Commission may administer oaths or affirmations to witnesses appearing before it.

(c) ACCESS TO INFORMATION.—The Commission may secure directly from any Federal agency information necessary to enable it to carry out this title, if the information may be disclosed under section 552 of title 5, United States Code. Subject to the previous sentence, on the request of the chairperson or vice chairperson of the Commission, the head of such agency shall furnish such information to the Commission.

(d) USE OF FACILITIES AND SERVICES.—Upon the request of the Commission, the head of any Federal agency may make available to the Commission any of the facilities and services of such agency.

(e) PERSONNEL FROM OTHER AGENCIES.—On the request of the Commission, the head of any Federal agency may detail any of the personnel of such agency to serve as an Executive Director of the Commission or assist the Commission in carrying out the duties of the Commission. Any detail shall not interrupt or otherwise affect the civil service status or privileges of the Federal employee.

(f) VOLUNTARY SERVICE.—Notwithstanding section 1342 of title 31, United States Code, the chairperson of the Commission may accept for the Commission voluntary services provided by a member of the Commission.

### SEC. 306. TERMINATION.

The Commission shall terminate 30 days after the date of the submission of the report of the Commission to Congress.

### TITLE IV—MISCELLANEOUS PROVISIONS

### SEC. 401. EFFECT ON OTHER LAWS.

(a) FEDERAL AND STATE ANTIDISCRIMINATION LAWS.—Nothing in this Act or any amendment made by this Act shall be construed to modify or affect any Federal or State law prohibiting discrimination on the basis of race, religion, color, national origin, sex, age, or disability.

(b) STATE AND LOCAL LAWS.—Nothing in this Act or any amendment made by this Act shall be construed to supersede any provision of any State or local law that provides greater family or medical leave rights than the rights established under this Act or any amendment made by this Act.

### SEC. 402. EFFECT ON EXISTING EMPLOYMENT BENEFITS.

(a) MORE PROTECTIVE.—Nothing in this Act or any amendment made by this Act shall be construed to diminish the obligation of an employer to comply with any collective bargaining agreement or any employment benefit program or plan that provides greater family or medical leave rights to employees than the rights established under this Act or any amendment made by this Act.

(b) LESS PROTECTIVE.—The rights established for employees under this Act or any amendment made by this Act shall not be diminished by any collective bargaining agreement or any employment benefit program or plan.

### SEC. 403. ENCOURAGEMENT OF MORE GENEROUS LEAVE POLICIES.

Nothing in this Act or any amendment made by this Act shall be construed to discourage employers from adopting or retaining leave policies more generous than any policies that comply with the requirements under this Act or any amendment made by this Act.

### SEC. 404. REGULATIONS.

The Secretary of Labor shall prescribe such regulations as are necessary to carry out title I and this title not later than 120 days after the date of the enactment of this Act.

### SEC. 405. EFFECTIVE DATES.

(a) TITLE III.—Title III shall take effect on the date of the enactment of this Act.

(b) OTHER TITLES.—

(1) IN GENERAL.—Except as provided in paragraph (2), titles I, II, and V and this title shall take effect 6 months after the date of the enactment of this Act.

(2) COLLECTIVE BARGAINING AGREEMENTS.—In the case of a collective bargaining agreement in effect on the effective date prescribed by paragraph (1), title I shall apply on the earlier of

(A) the date of the termination of such agreement; or

(B) the date that occurs 12 months after the date of the enactment of this Act.

## TITLE V—COVERAGE OF CONGRESSIONAL EMPLOYEES

### SEC. 501. LEAVE FOR CERTAIN SENATE EMPLOYEES.

(a) COVERAGE.—The rights and protections established under sections 101 through 105 shall apply with respect to a Senate employee and an employing office. For purposes of such application, the term "eligible employee" means a Senate employee and the term "employer" means an employing office.

(b) CONSIDERATION OF ALLEGATIONS.

(1) APPLICABLE PROVISIONS.—The provisions of sections 304 through 313 of the Government Employee Rights Act of 1991 (2 U.S.C. 1204-1213) shall, except as provided in subsections (d) and (e)—

(A) apply with respect to an allegation of a violation of a provision of sections 101 through 105, with respect to Senate employment of a Senate employee; and

(B) apply to such an allegation in the same manner and to the same extent as such sections of the Government Employee Rights Act of 1991 apply with respect to an allegation of a violation under such Act.

(2) ENTITY.—Such an allegation shall be addressed by the Office of Senate Fair Employment Practices or such other entity as the Senate may designate.

(c) RIGHTS OF EMPLOYEES.—The Office of Senate Fair Employment Practices shall ensure that Senate employees are informed of their rights under sections 101 through 105.

(d) LIMITATIONS.—A request for counseling under section 305 of such Act by a Senate employee alleging a violation of a provision of sections 101 through 105 shall be made not later than 2 years after the date of the last event constituting the alleged violation for which the counseling is requested, or not later than 3 years after such date in the case of a willful violation of section 105.

(e) APPLICABLE REMEDIES.—The remedies applicable to individuals who demonstrate a violation of a provision of sections 101 through 105 shall be such remedies as would be appropriate if awarded under paragraph (1) or (3) of section 107(a).

(f) EXERCISE OF RULEMAKING POWER.—The provisions of subsections (b), (c), (d), and (e), except as such subsections apply with respect to section 309 of the Government Employee Rights Act of 1991 (2 U.S.C. 1209), are enacted by the Senate as an exercise of the rulemaking power of the Senate, with full recognition of the right of the Senate to change its rules, in the same manner, and to the same extent, as in the case of any other rule of the Senate. No Senate employee may commence a judicial proceeding with respect to an allegation described in subsection (b)(1), except as provided in this section.

(g) SEVERABILITY.—Notwithstanding any other provision of law, if any provision of section 309 of the Government Employee Rights Act of 1991 (2 U.S.C. 1209), or of subsection (b)(1) insofar as it applies such section 309 to an allegation described in subsection (b)(1)(A), is invalidated, both such section 309, and subsection (b)(1) insofar as it applies such section 309 to such an allegation, shall have no force and effect, and shall be considered to be invalidated for purposes of section 322 of such Act (2 U.S.C. 1221).

(h) DEFINITIONS.—As used in this section:

(1) EMPLOYING OFFICE.—The term "employing office" means the office with the final authority described in section 301(2) of such Act (2 U.S.C. 1201(2)).

(2) SENATE EMPLOYEE.—The term "Senate employee" means an employee described in subparagraph (A) or (B) of section 301(c)(1) of such Act (2 U.S.C. 1201(c)(1)) who has been employed for at least 12 months on other than a temporary or intermittent basis by any employing office.

### SEC. 502. LEAVE FOR CERTAIN HOUSE EMPLOYEES.

(a) IN GENERAL.—The rights and protections under sections 102 through 105 (other than section 104(b)) shall apply to any employee in an employment position and any employing authority of the House of Representatives.

(b) ADMINISTRATION.—In the administration of this section, the remedies and procedures under the Fair Employment Practices Resolution shall be applied.

(c) DEFINITION.—As used in this section, the term "Fair Employment Practices Resolution" means rule LI of the Rules of the House of Representatives.

## TITLE VI—SENSE OF CONGRESS

### SEC. 601. SENSE OF CONGRESS.

It is the sense of the Congress that:

(a) The Secretary of Defense shall conduct a comprehensive review of current departmental policy with respect to the service of homosexuals in the Armed Forces;

(b) Such review shall include the basis for the current policy of mandatory separation; the rights of all service men and women, and the effects of any change in such policy on morale, discipline, and military effectiveness;

(c) The Secretary shall report the results of such review and consultations and his recommendations to the President and to the Congress no later than July 15, 1993;

(d) The Senate Committee on Armed Services shall conduct (i) comprehensive hearings on the current military policy with respect to the service of homosexuals in the military services; and (ii) shall conduct oversight hearings on the Secretary's recommendations as such are reported.

# APPENDIX 2:
# EMPLOYER RESPONSE TO EMPLOYEE REQUEST FOR FAMILY OR MEDICAL LEAVE [DOL FORM WH-381]

Employer Response to Employee
Request for Family or Medical Leave
(Optional Use Form -- See 29 CFR § 825.301)

**U.S. Department of Labor**
Employment Standards Administration
Wage and Hour Division

**(Family and Medical Leave Act of 1993)**

OMB No. : 1215-0181
Expires : 08-31-07

Date:

To: _____
(Employee's Name)

From: _____
(Name of Appropriate Employer Representative)

**Subject: REQUEST FOR FAMILY/MEDICAL LEAVE**

On _____ , you notified us of your need to take family/medical leave due to:
(Date)

    The birth of a child, or the placement of a child with you for adoption or foster care; or

    A serious health condition that makes you unable to perform the essential functions for your job: or

    A serious health condition affecting your     spouse,     child,     parent, for which you are needed to provide care.

You notified us that you need this leave beginning on _____ and that you expect
(Date)
leave to continue until on or about _____ .
(Date)

Except as explained below, you have a right under the FMLA for up to 12 weeks of unpaid leave in a 12-month period for the reasons listed above. Also, your health benefits must be maintained during any period of unpaid leave under the same conditions as if you continued to work, and you must be reinstated to the same or an equivalent job with the same pay, benefits, and terms and conditions of employment on your return from leave. If you do not return to work following FMLA leave for a reason other than: (1) the continuation, recurrence, or onset of a serious health condition which would entitle you to FMLA leave; or (2) other circumstances beyond your control, you may be required to reimburse us for our share of health insurance premiums paid on your behalf during your FMLA leave.

This is to inform you that: *(check appropriate boxes; explain where indicated)*

1. You are    eligible    not eligible for leave under the FMLA.

2. The requested leave    will    will not be counted against your annual FMLA leave entitlement.

3. You    will    will not be required to furnish medical certification of a serious health condition. If required, you must furnish certification by _____ *(insert date)* (must be at least 15 days after you are notified of this requirement), or we may delay the commencement of your leave until the certification is submitted.

4. You may elect to substitute accrued paid leave for unpaid FMLA leave. We    will    will not require that you substitute accrued paid leave for unpaid FMLA leave. If paid leave will be used, the following conditions will apply: *(Explain)*

Form WH-381
Rev. June 1997

5. (a) If you normally pay a portion of the premiums for your health insurance, these payments will continue during the period of FMLA leave. Arrangements for payment have been discussed with you, and it is agreed that you will make premium payments as follows: *(Set forth dates, e.g., the 10th of each month, or payperiods, etc. that specifically cover the agreement with the employee.)*

(b) You have a minimum 30-day *(or, indicate longer period, if applicable)* grace period in which to make premium payments. If payment is not made timely, your group health insurance may be cancelled, *provided* we notify you in writing at least 15 days before the date that your health coverage will lapse, or, at our option, we may pay your share of the premiums during FMLA leave, and recover these payments from you upon your return to work. We _____ will _____ will not pay your share of health insurance premiums while you are on leave.

(c) We _____ will _____ will not do the same with other benefits *(e.g., life insurance, disability insurance, etc.)* while you are on FMLA leave. If we do pay your premiums for other benefits, when you return from leave you _____ will _____ will not be expected to reimburse us for the payments made on your behalf.

6. You _____ will _____ will not be required to present a fitness-for-duty certificate prior to being restored to employment. If such certification is required but not received, your return to work may be delayed until certification is provided.

7. (a) You _____ are _____ are not a "key employee" as described in § 825.217 of the FMLA regulations. If you are a "key employee:" restoration to employment may be denied following FMLA leave on the grounds that such restoration will cause substantial and grievous economic injury to us as discussed in § 825.218.

(b) We _____ have _____ have not determined that restoring you to employment at the conclusion of FMLA leave will cause substantial and grievous economic harm to *us. (Explain (a) and/or (b) below. See §825.219 of the FMLA regulations.)*

8. While on leave, you _____ will _____ will not be required to furnish us with periodic reports every _____ _____ *(indicate interval of periodic reports, as appropriate for the particular leave situation)* of your status and intent to return to work *(see § 825.309 of the FMLA regulations).* If the circumstances of your leave change and you are able to return to work earlier than the date indicated on the reverse side of this form, you _____ will _____ will not be required to notify us at least two work days prior to the date you intend to report to work.

9. You _____ will _____ will not be required to furnish recertification relating to a serious health condition. *(Explain below. if necessary, including the interval between certifications as prescribed in §825.308 of the FMLA regulations.)*

This optional use form may be used to satisfy mandatory employer requirements to provide employees taking FMLA leave with Written notice detailing specific expectations and obligations of the employee and explaining any consequences of a failure to meet these obligations. (29 CFR 825.301(b).)

*Note:* Persons are not required to respond to this collection of information unless it displays a currently valid OMB control number.

**Public Burden Statement**

We estimate that it will take an average of 5 minutes to complete this collection of information, including the time for reviewing instructions. searching existing data sources, gathering and maintaining the data needed, and completing and reviewing the collection of information. If you have any comments regarding this burden estimate or any other aspect of this collection of information, including suggestions for reducing this burden. send them to the Administrator, Wage and Hour Division, Department of Labor, Room S-3502. 200 Constitution Avenue, N.W., Washington. D.C. 20210.

DO NOT SEND THE COMPLETED FORM TO THE OFFICE SHOWN ABOVE.

# APPENDIX 3:
# CERTIFICATION OF HEALTH CARE
# PROVIDER [DOL FORM WHL-380]

Certification of Health Care Provider
(Family and Medical Leave Act of 1993)

**U.S. Department of Labor**
Employment Standards Administration
Wage and Hour Division

*(When completed, this form goes to the employee, **Not to the Department of Labor**.)*

OMB No.: 1215-0181
Expires: 07/31/07

1. Employee's Name

2. Patient's Name *(If different from employee)*

3. Page 4 describes what is meant by a **"serious health condition"** under the Family and Medical Leave Act. Does the patient's condition[1] qualify under any of the categories described? If so, please check the applicable category.

   (1) _____ (2) _____ (3) _____ (4) _____ (5) _____ (6) _____ , or None of the above _____

4. Describe the **medical facts** which support your certification, including a brief statement as to how the medical facts meet the criteria of one of these categories:

5. a. State the approximate **date** the condition commenced, and the probable duration of the condition (and also the probable duration of the patient's present **incapacity**[2] if different):

   b. Will it be necessary for the employee to take work only **intermittently or to work on a less than full schedule** as a result of the condition (including for treatment described in Item 6 below)?

   If yes, give the probable duration:

   c. If the condition is a **chronic condition** (condition #4) or **pregnancy**, state whether the patient is presently incapacitated[2] and the likely duration and frequency of **episodes of incapacity**[2]:

[1] Here and elsewhere on this form, the information sought relates **only** to the condition for which the employee is taking FMLA leave.

[2] "Incapacity," for purposes of FMLA, is defined to mean inability to work, attend school or perform other regular daily activities due to the serious health condition, treatment therefor, or recovery therefrom.

Page 1 of 4

Form WH-380
Revised December 1999

---

6. a. If additional **treatments** will be required for the condition, provide an estimate of the probable number of such treatments.

   If the patient will be absent from work or other daily activities because of **treatment** on an **intermittent** or **part-time** basis, also provide an estimate of the probable number of and interval between such treatments, actual or estimated dates of treatment if known, and period required for recovery if any:

   b. If any of these treatments will be provided by **another provider of health services** (e.g., physical therapist), please state the nature of the treatments:

   c. **If a regimen of continuing treatment** by the patient is required under your supervision, provide a general description of such regimen (*e.g.*, prescription drugs, physical therapy requiring special equipment):

7. a. If medical leave is required for the employee's **absence from work** because of the **employee's own condition** (including absences due to pregnancy or a chronic condition), is the employee **unable to perform work** of any kind?

   b. If able to perform some work, is the employee **unable to perform any one or more of the essential functions of the employee's job** (the employee or the employer should supply you with information about the essential job functions)? If yes, please list the essential functions the employee is unable to perform:

   c. If neither a. nor b. applies, is it necessary for the employee to be **absent from work for treatment**?

Page 2 of 4

8. a. If leave is required to **care for a family member** of the employee with a serious health condition, **does the patient require assistance** for basic medical or personal needs or safety, or for transportation?

b. If no, would the employee's presence to provide **psychological comfort** be beneficial to the patient or assist in the patient's recovery?

c. If the patient will need care only **intermittently** or on a part-time basis, please indicate the probable **duration** of this need:

Signature of Health Care Provider

Type of Practice

Address

Telephone Number

Date

**To be completed by the employee needing family leave to care for a family member:**

State the care you will provide and an estimate of the period during which care will be provided, including a schedule if leave is to be taken intermittently or if it will be necessary for you to work less than a full schedule:

Employee Signature

Date

Page 3 of 4

A **"Serious Health Condition"** means an illness, injury impairment, or physical or mental condition that involves one of the following:

1. Hospital Care

   **Inpatient care** (*i.e.*, an overnight stay) in a hospital, hospice, or residential medical care facility, including any period of incapacity[2] or subsequent treatment in connection with or consequent to such inpatient care.

2. Absence Plus Treatment

   (a) A period of incapacity[2] of **more than three consecutive calendar days** (including any subsequent treatment or period of incapacity[2] relating to the same condition), that also involves:

      (1) **Treatment**[3] **two or more times** by a health care provider, by a nurse or physician's assistant under direct supervision of a health care provider, or by a provider of health care services (*e.g.*, physical therapist) under orders of, or on referral by, a health care provider; or

      (2) **Treatment** by a health care provider on **at least one occasion** which results in a **regimen of continuing treatment**[4] under the supervision of the health care provider.

3. Pregnancy

   Any period of incapacity due to **pregnancy**, or for **prenatal care**.

4. Chronic Conditions Requiring Treatments

   A **chronic condition** which:

      (1) Requires **periodic visits** for treatment by a health care provider, or by a nurse or physician's assistant under direct supervision of a health care provider;

      (2) Continues over an **extended period of time** (including recurring episodes of a single underlying condition); and

      (3) May cause **episodic** rather than a continuing period of incapacity[2] (*e.g.*, asthma, diabetes, epilepsy, etc.).

5. Permanent/Long-term Conditions Requiring Supervision

   A period of **Incapacity**[2] which is **permanent or long-term** due to a condition for which treatment may not be effective. The employee or family member must be **under the continuing supervision of, but need not be receiving active treatment by, a health care provider**. Examples include Alzheimer's, a severe stroke, or the terminal stages of a disease.

6. Multiple Treatments (Non-Chronic Conditions)

   Any period of absence to receive **multiple treatments** (including any period of recovery therefrom) by a health care provider or by a provider of health care services under orders of, or on referral by, a health care provider, either for **restorative surgery** after an accident or other injury, **or** for a condition that **would likely result in a period of Incapacity**[2] **of more than three consecutive calendar days in the absence of medical intervention or treatment,** such as cancer (chemotherapy, radiation, etc.), severe arthritis (physical therapy), and kidney disease (dialysis).

This optional form may be used by employees to satisfy a mandatory requirement to furnish a medical certification (when requested) from a health care provider, including second or third opinions and recertification (29 CFR 825.306).

*Note:* Persons are not required to respond to this collection of information unless it displays a currently valid OMB control number.

[3] Treatment includes examinations to determine if a serious health condition exists and evaluations of the condition. Treatment does not include routine physical examinations, eye examinations, or dental examinations.

[4] A regimen of continuing treatment includes, for example, a course of prescription medication (*e.g.*, an antibiotic) or therapy requiring special equipment to resolve or alleviate the health condition. A regimen of treatment does not include the taking of over-the-counter medications such as aspirin, antihistamines, or salves; or bed-rest, drinking fluids, exercise, and other similar activities that can be initiated without a visit to a health care provider.

**Public Burden Statement**

We estimate that it will take an average of 20 minutes to complete this collection of information, including the time for reviewing instructions, searching existing data sources, gathering and maintaining the data needed, and completing and reviewing the collection of information. If you have any comments regarding this burden estimate or any other aspect of this collection of information, including suggestions for reducing this burden, send them to the Administrator, Wage and Hour Division, Department of Labor, Room S-3502, 200 Constitution Avenue, N.W., Washington, D.C. 20210.

*DO NOT SEND THE COMPLETED FORM TO THIS OFFICE; IT GOES TO THE EMPLOYEE.*

# APPENDIX 4:
# "FMLA POSTER—YOUR RIGHTS UNDER THE FAMILY AND MEDICAL LEAVE ACT OF 1993"

## Your Rights
### under the
## Family and Medical Leave Act of 1993

FMLA requires covered employers to provide up to 12 weeks of unpaid, job-protected leave to "eligible" employees for certain family and medical reasons. Employees are eligible if they have worked for their employer for at least one year, and for 1,250 hours over the previous 12 months, and if there are at least 50 employees within 75 miles. The FMLA permits employees to take leave on an intermittent basis or to work a reduced schedule under certain circumstances.

### Reasons for Taking Leave:

Unpaid leave must be granted for *any* of the following reasons:

- to care for the employee's child after birth, or placement for adoption or foster care;
- to care for the employee's spouse, son or daughter, or parent who has a serious health condition; or
- for a serious health condition that makes the employee unable to perform the employee's job.

At the employee's or employer's option, certain kinds of *paid* leave may be substituted for unpaid leave.

### Advance Notice and Medical Certification:

The employee may be required to provide advance leave notice and medical certification. Taking of leave may be denied if requirements are not met.

- The employee ordinarily must provide 30 days advance notice when the leave is "foreseeable."
- An employer may require medical certification to support a request for leave because of a serious health condition, and may require second or third opinions (at the employer's expense) and a fitness for duty report to return to work.

### Job Benefits and Protection:

- For the duration of FMLA leave, the employer must maintain the employee's health coverage under any "group health plan."

- Upon return from FMLA leave, most employees must be restored to their original or equivalent positions with equivalent pay, benefits, and other employment terms.
- The use of FMLA leave cannot result in the loss of any employment benefit that accrued prior to the start of an employee's leave.

### Unlawful Acts by Employers:

FMLA makes it unlawful for any employer to:

- interfere with, restrain, or deny the exercise of any right provided under FMLA:
- discharge or discriminate against any person for opposing any practice made unlawful by FMLA or for involvement in any proceeding under or relating to FMLA.

### Enforcement:

- The U.S. Department of Labor is authorized to investigate and resolve complaints of violations.
- An eligible employee may bring a civil action against an employer for violations.

FMLA does not affect any Federal or State law prohibiting discrimination, or supersede any State or local law or collective bargaining agreement which provides greater family or medical leave rights.

### For Additional Information:

If you have access to the Internet visit our FMLA website: http://www.dol.gov/esa/whd/fmla. To locate your nearest Wage-Hour Office, telephone our Wage-Hour toll-free information and help line at 1-866-4USWAGE (1-866-487-9243): a customer service representative is available to assist you with referral information from 8am to 5pm **in your time zone;** or log onto our Home Page at http://www.wagehour.dol.gov.

U.S. Department of Labor
Employment Standards Administration
Wage and Hour Division
Washington, D.C. 20210

WH Publication 1420
Revised August 2001

*U.S. GOVERNMENT PRINTING OFFICE 2001-476-344/49051

# APPENDIX 5:
## DIRECTORY OF STATE DEPARTMENTS OF LABOR

| STATE | ADDRESS | TELEPHONE | FAX | WEBSITE |
|-------|---------|-----------|-----|---------|
| Alabama | Department of Labor<br>P.O. Box 303500<br>Montgomery, AL 36130-3500 | 334-242-3460 | 334-240-3417 | N/A |
| Alaska | Department of Labor and<br>Workforce Development<br>P.O. Box 21149<br>Juneau, AK 99801-1149 | 907-465-2700 | 907-465-2784 | www.labor.state.ak.us |
| Arizona | State Labor Department<br>P.O. Box 19070<br>Phoenix, AZ 85005-9070 | 602-542-4515 | 602-542-8097 | www.ica.state.az.us |

| STATE | ADDRESS | TELEPHONE | FAX | WEBSITE |
|---|---|---|---|---|
| Arkansas | Department of Labor 10421 West Markham Little Rock, AR 72205 | 501-682-4541 | 501-682-4535 | www.state.ar.us/labor |
| California | State Labor Commissioner, Division of Labor Standards Enforcement 455 Golden Gate Ave., 9th Floor San Francisco, CA 94102 | 415-703-4810 | 415-703-4807 | www.dir.ca.gov |
| Colorado | Labor Standards Office 1515 Arapahoe Street, Suite 375 Denver, CO 80202-2117 | 303-318-8468 | 303-318-8400 | http://www.coworkforce.com |
| Connecticut | Labor Department 200 Folly Brook Boulevard Wethersfield, CT 06109-1114 | 860-263-6505 | 860-263-6529 | www.ctdol.state.ct.us |
| Delaware | Department of Labor 4425 N. Market Street, 4th Floor Wilmington, DE 19802 | 302-761-8000 | 302-761-6621 | www.delawareworks.com |
| District of Columbia | Department of Employment Services 54 New York Ave. NE, Suite 3007 Washington, D.C. 20002 | 202-671-1900 | 202-673-6993 | N/A |
| Florida | Agency for Workforce Innovation Caldwell Bldg., Suite 100 107 East Madison St., Tallahassee, FL 32399-4120 | 850-245-7105 | 850-921-3223 | http://www.floridajobs.org/ or http://www.MyFlorida.com |

| STATE | ADDRESS | TELEPHONE | FAX | WEBSITE |
|---|---|---|---|---|
| Georgia | Department of Labor Sussex Place—Room 600, 148 International Blvd. N.E. Atlanta, GA 3030 | 404-656-3011 | 404-656-2683 | www.dol.state.ga.us |
| Hawaii | Department of Labor and Industrial Relations 830 Punchbowl Street Room 321 Honolulu, HI 96813 | 808-586-8865 | 808-586-9099 | www.dlir.state.hi.us |
| Idaho | Department of Labor, 317 W. Main Street, Boise, ID 83735-0001 | 208-332-3579 | 208-334-6430 | www.labor.state.id.us |
| Illinois | Department of Labor 160 N. LaSalle Street, 13th Floor Suite C-1300, Chicago, IL 60601 | 312-793-1808 | 312-793-5257 | www.state.il.us/agency/idol |
| Indiana | Department of Labor, Indiana Government Center South 402 West Washington Street Room W195, Indianapolis, IN 46204-2739 | 317-232-2378 | 317-233-5381 | www.state.in.us/labor |
| Iowa | Division of Labor Services 1000 East Grand Avenue Des Moines, IA 50319 | 515-281-3447 | 515-281-4698 | www.iowaworkforce.org/labor |
| Kansas | Department of Human Resources 401 S.W. Topeka Boulevard Topeka, KS 66603-3182 | 785-296-7474 | 785-368-6294 | www2.hr.state.ks.us |

| STATE | ADDRESS | TELEPHONE | FAX | WEBSITE |
|---|---|---|---|---|
| Kentucky | Department of Labor<br>1047 U.S. Hwy.<br>127 South, Suite 4<br>Frankfort, KY 40601-4381 | 502-564-3070 | 502-564-5387 | www.kylabor.net |
| Louisiana | Department of Labor<br>P.O. Box 94094<br>Baton Rouge, LA 70804-9094 | 225-342-3011 | 225-342-3778 | www.ldol.state.la.us |
| Maine | Department of Labor<br>State House Station #45<br>Augusta, ME 04333-0045 | 207-624-6400 | 207-624-6449 | http://www.state.me.us/labor |
| Maryland | Department of Labor<br>Division of Workforce<br>Development<br>1100 Eutaw St.—6th Floor<br>Baltimore, MD 21201 | 410-767-2999 | 410-767-2986 | www.dllr.state.md.us |
| Massachusetts | Department of Labor & Work<br>Force Development<br>1 Ashburton Place, Rm 2112<br>Boston, MA 02108 | 617-727-6573 | 617-727-1090 | www.mass.gov/dlwd |
| Michigan | Department of Labor and<br>Economic Growth<br>P.O. Box 30004<br>Lansing, MI 48909 | 517-373-3034 | 517-373-2129 | www.michigan.gov/bwuc |

| STATE | ADDRESS | TELEPHONE | FAX | WEBSITE |
|---|---|---|---|---|
| Minnesota | Department of Labor and Industry<br>443 Lafayette Road<br>St. Paul, MN 55155 | 651-284-5010 | 651-284-5721 | www.doli.state.mn.us |
| Mississippi | Department of Employment Security<br>P.O. Box 1699<br>Jackson, MS 39215-1699 | 601-321-6100 | 601-321-610 | www.mesc.state.ms.us |
| Missouri | Labor and Industrial Relations Commission<br>3315 W. Truman Boulevard<br>Jefferson City, MO 65102-0599 | 573-751-2461 | 573-751-7806 | N/A |
| Montana | Department of Labor and Industry<br>P.O. Box 1728<br>Helena, MT 59624-1728 | 406-444-9091 | 406-444-1394 | http://dli.state.mt.us |
| Nebraska | Department of Labor<br>550 South 16th Street<br>P.O. Box 94600<br>Lincoln, NE 68509-4600 | 402-471-3405 | 402-471-2318 | www.dol.state.ne.us/ |
| Nevada | Department of Business and Industry<br>555 E. Washington Avenue<br>Suite 4100<br>Las Vegas, NV 89101-1050 | 702-486-2650 | 702-486-2660 | www.LaborCommissioner.com or<br>http://dbi.state.nv.us |

| STATE | ADDRESS | TELEPHONE | FAX | WEBSITE |
|---|---|---|---|---|
| New Hampshire | Department of Labor<br>95 Pleasant Street<br>Concord, NH 03301 | 603-271-3171 | 603-271-6852 | www.labor.state.nh.us |
| New Jersey | Department of Labor<br>John Fitch Plaza, 13th Floor<br>Suite D<br>P.O. Box 110<br>Trenton, NJ 08625-0110 | 609-292-2323 | 609-633-9271 | www.state.nj.us/labor/index.html \ |
| New Mexico | Department of Labor<br>P.O. Box 1928<br>401 Broadway N.E.<br>Albuquerque, NM 87103-1928 | 505-841-8409 | 505-841-8491 | www3.state.nm.us/dol/dol_home.html |
| New York | Department of Labor<br>State Campus, Building 12<br>Room 500<br>Albany, NY 12240-0003 | 518-457-2741 | 518-457-6908 | www.labor.state.ny.us |
| North Carolina | Department of Labor<br>4 West Edenton Street<br>Raleigh, NC 27601-1092 | 919-733-0359 | 919-733-0223 | www.nclabor.com |
| North Dakota | Department of Labor<br>State Capitol Building<br>600 East Boulevard,,Dept. 406<br>Bismarck,. ND 58505-0340 | 701-328-2660 | 701-328-2031 | www.state.nd.us/labor/ |

| STATE | ADDRESS | TELEPHONE | FAX | WEBSITE |
|---|---|---|---|---|
| Ohio | Division of Labor and Worker Safety 50 West Broad St., 28th Floor Columbus, OH 43215 | 614-644-2239 | 614-728-8639-5650 | http://www.state.oh.us/ohio/agency.htm |
| Oklahoma | Department of Labor, 4001 N. Lincoln Blvd. Oklahoma City, OK 73105-5212 | 405-528-150, ext. 2000 | 405-528-5751 | www.state.ok.us/~okdol |
| Oregon | Bureau of Labor and Industries 800 NE Oregon Street #32 Portland, OR 97232 | 503-731-4070 | 503-731-4103 | www.boli.state.or.us |
| Pennsylvania | Department of Labor and Industry 1700 Labor and Industry Building, 7th and Forster Streets Harrisburg, PA 17120 | 717-787-5279 | 717-787-8826 | www.dli.state.pa.us |
| Rhode Island | Department of Labor and Training 1511 Pontiac Avenue Cranston, RI 02920 | 401-462-8870 | 401-462-8872 | www.det.state.ri.us |
| South Carolina | Department of Labor Synergy Center Kingstree Building 110 Center View Drive P.O.Box 11329 Columbia, SC 29211-1329 | 803-896-4300 | 803-896-4393 | www.llr.state.sc.us |

| STATE | ADDRESS | TELEPHONE | FAX | WEBSITE |
|---|---|---|---|---|
| South Dakota | Department of Labor 700 Governors Drive Pierre, SD 57501-2291 | 605-773-3101 | 605-773-4211 | www.state.sd.us/dol/dol.htm |
| Tennessee | Department of Labor Andrew Johnson Tower 710 James Robertson Pky. 8th Floor Nashville, TN 37243-0655 | 615-741-6642 | 615-741-5078 | Internet:www.state.tn.us/labor-wfd/ |
| Texas | Texas Workforce Commission 101 East 15th Street., Rm 67 Austin, TX 78778 | 512-463-2829 | 512-475-2152 | www.twc.state.tx.us |
| Utah | Labor Commission P.O. Box 146610 Salt Lake City, UT 84114-6610 | 801-530-6880 | 801-530-6804 | www.labor.state.ut.us |
| Vermont | Department of Labor & Industry National Life Building, Drawer #20 Montpelier, VT 05620-3401 | 802-828-2288 | 802-828-0408 | www.state.vt.us/labind |
| Virginia | Department of Labor and Industry Powers-Taylor Building, 13 S. 13th St. Richmond, VA 23219 | 804-786-2377 | 804-371-6524 | www.dli.state.va.us |
| Washington | Department of Labor & Industries P.O. Box 44001 Olympia, WA 98504-4001 | 360-902-4203 | 360-902-4202 | www.lni.wa.gov |

| STATE | ADDRESS | TELEPHONE | FAX | WEBSITE |
|-------|---------|-----------|-----|---------|
| West Virginia | Division of Labor State Capitol Complex Building #6, Room B749 Charleston, WV 25305 | 304-558-7890 | 304-558-3797 | www.state.wv.us/labor |
| Wisconsin | Department of Workforce Development 201 East Washington Avenue # A400 P.O. Box 7946 Madison, WI 53707-7946 | 608-267-9692 | 608-266-1784 | www.dwd.state.wi.us |
| Wyoming | Department of Employment 1510 E Pershing, West Wing Cheyenne, WY 82002 | 307-777-7261 | 307-777-5633 | http://wydoe.state.wy.us |

# APPENDIX 6:
# FEDERAL/STATE FMLA COMPARISON CHART

*PROVISION: COVERED EMPLOYERS*

FEDERAL: Private Employers of 50 or more Employees in at least 20 weeks of the current or preceding year; Public agencies, including state, local, and Federal Employers; Local education agencies covered under special provisions

CALIFORNIA: Anyone who directly employs 50 or more Employees; The state and any political or civil subdivision of the state and cities; No special provision for education agencies

CONNECTICUT: Private sector Employers of 75 or more Employees, determined as of October 1 annually, excepting private or parochial elementary or secondary schools; State agencies covered under separate statute, with similar provisions; Local government agencies, including local education agencies, excepted

DISTRICT OF COLUMBIA: Any individual, firm, association, corporation, the D.C. government, receiver or trustee of any individual, firm, association, or corporation, or the legal representative of a deceased Employer who uses the services of an individual for pay in the District; Local education agencies subject to special provisions

HAWAII: Employees of the State, its political subdivisions, and its instrumentalities were no longer included under the protections provided by the state statute, but they remain protected under the provisions of the Federal statute); No special provision for education agencies

MAINE: Any business entity that employs 15 or more Employees at one location in this State; The State, all branches, departments or agencies; Any city, town or municipal agency that employs 25 or more Employees; Any agent of an Employer, the State or political subdivision; No special provision for local education agencies

MINNESOTA: Employers of 21 or more Employees located at least at one worksite and includes a corporation, partnership, association, nonprofit organization, group of persons, state, county, town, city, school district, or other governmental subdivision; No special provision for education agencies; For limited parental leave to attend school conferences and activities, Employer includes any entity with one or more Employees

NEW JERSEY: Public and private Employers of 50 or more Employees each working day during each of 20 or more calendar workweeks in the then current or immediately preceding calendar year; includes the State, any political subdivision thereof, and all public offices, agencies, boards or bodies; No special provision for education agencies

OREGON: Employers with 25 or more Employees in the State of Oregon for each working day during each of 20 or more calendar workweeks of the current or preceding year, but excepting employers meeting certain conditions and providing family leave at least as generous as required by statute; Special provisions for teachers

RHODE ISLAND: Private Employers of 50 or more Employees; Any State agency. Any city, town, or municipal agency that employs 30 or more Employees; No special provision for education agencies

VERMONT: Private and public Employers of 10 or more for purposes of parental leave; Private and public Employers of 15 or more for purposes of family leave; No special provision for education agencies

WASHINGTON: Private Employers and units of local government who have employed a daily average of 100 or more Employees during the last calendar quarter within a 20 mile radius of the place where the Employee requesting leave reports for work, or the Employer employed a daily average of 100 Employees during the last calendar quarter within 20 miles of where the requesting Employee reports for work, where the Employer maintains a central hiring location and customarily transfers the workers among workplaces; All State agencies; No special provision for education agencies

WISCONSIN: Private and public Employers with at least 50 individuals on a permanent basis; No special provision for education agencies

## *PROVISION: EMPLOYEES ELIGIBLE*

FEDERAL: Worked for Employer for at least 12 months—which need not be consecutive; worked at least 1,250 hours for Employer during 12 months preceding leave; and employed at Employer worksite with 50 or more Employees or within 75 miles of Employer worksites with a total of 50 or more Employees

CALIFORNIA: Similar to Federal provision, including worksite proviso

CONNECTICUT: 1000 hours service with Employer during 12-month period preceding first day of leave; No worksite proviso

DISTRICT OF COLUMBIA: Have worked for one year with same Employer without a break in service except for regular holidays, sick or personal leave granted by Employer with at least 1000 hours service during the past 12-month period prior to leave request; No worksite proviso

HAWAII: Employees who have worked for 6 consecutive months; No worksite proviso

MAINE: Any Employee employed by same Employer for 12 consecutive months at a permanent worksite with 15 or more Employees

MINNESOTA: Employed for at least 12 consecutive months prior to leave request; Employee worked for Employer for an average number of hours equal to one-half the full-time equivalent position in the Employee's job classification in the preceding 12 months; No worksite proviso

NEW JERSEY: 12 months with an Employer for not less than 1000 base hours during the immediately preceding 12 months; No worksite proviso

OREGON: Have worked average of 25 or more hours/week and employed 180 days for an Employer immediately preceding commencement of leave in order to qualify for family leave. The only requirement for parental leave is to have been employed for 180 days immediately preceding the commencement of leave; No worksite proviso

RHODE ISLAND: Any full-time Employees working on average 30 or more hours per week for 12 consecutive months (1560 hours); No worksite proviso

VERMONT: Employees worked an average of 30 hours per week for one year; No worksite proviso

WASHINGTON: Employed by the Employer on a continuous basis for the previous 52 weeks for at least 35 hours per week; See above for worksite proviso

WISCONSIN: Have worked for Employer for at least 52 consecutive weeks and at least 1000 hours in preceding 52 weeks; No worksite proviso

## PROVISION: LEAVE AMOUNT

FEDERAL: Up to a total of 12 weeks during a 12-month period; however, leave for birth, adoption, foster care, or to care for a parent with a serious health condition must be shared by spouses working for same Employer

CALIFORNIA: Similar to Federal provision; Under separate statute, State Employees may receive up to 12-months leave for pregnancy, childbirth, or adoption, or care for newborn; No requirement that spouses share leave. Under separate statute, employers are required to provide a female employee affected by pregnancy, childbirth, or related medical condition the same benefits as provided employees on temporary disability (for a period of 6 weeks or less). An employee also is entitled to take pregnancy leave for a reasonable period of time not to exceed 4 months.

CONNECTICUT: Employees of covered Employers may receive 16 weeks of leave in a 24 month period; State employees in the state are entitled to a maximum of 24 weeks of medical leave in any two (2) year period in order to serve as an organ or bone marrow donor; Similar to Federal provision regarding sharing of leave by spouses

DISTRICT OF COLUMBIA: 16 weeks during 24-month period for family leave (care for family member); 16 weeks for medical leave (employee's own serious health condition); Leave rights for birth or placement expire 12 months after birth of child or placement; Leave must be shared by family members working for the same Employer

HAWAII: Up to 4 weeks during any calendar year; No provision requiring spouses to share leave

MAINE: 10 weeks during a 2-year period; No provision regarding spousal sharing of leave

MINNESOTA: Up to 6 weeks for birth or adoption (unless Employee and Employer agree to longer period); May use personal sick leave benefits to attend to a child for a reasonable period of time; No provision regarding spousal sharing of leave

NEW JERSEY: 12 weeks in any 24-month period; No provision requiring spouses to share leave

OREGON: 12 weeks within any one-year period. Additional leave may be available in some circumstances. See below.

RHODE ISLAND: 13 consecutive weeks in any 2 calendar years

VERMONT: 12 weeks in a 12-month period for family or parental leave, i.e., serious illness of the Employee or the Employee's child, stepchild or ward of the Employee who lives with the Employee, parent, spouse, or parent of Employee's spouse; birth of the Employee's child or adoption placement; Additionally, Employees are allowed "short-time family leave," 4 hours in any 30-day period and not to exceed 24 hours in any 12-month period in order to respond to a medical emergency involving the Employee's child or ward who lives with the Employee or the Employee's parent, spouse, or parent-in-law. This leave may also be used for certain preschool or school activities, routine medical and dental appointments, or other professional services related to their well-being; No provision requiring spouses to share leave; Employee permitted to waive any or all rights by informed, voluntary agreement with Employer

WASHINGTON: 12 weeks within 24 months, but note that FMLA leave shall be in addition to any leave because of childbirth or illness during pregnancy; Spouses required to share leave

WISCONSIN: During a 12-month period: (1) 6 weeks for a birth or adoption; (2) 2 weeks for serious health condition of parent, step-parent, child or spouse; (3) 2 weeks for Employee's own serious health condition; (4) Employee may not take more than 8 weeks in a year for any combination of the above leave; No provision requiring spouses to share leave

### PROVISION: TYPE OF LEAVE

---

FEDERAL: Unpaid leave for birth, placement of child for adoption or foster care, to provide care for Employee's own parent (including individuals who exercise parental responsibility under state law), child under 18 or a dependant adult child, or spouse with serious health condition, or Employee's own serious health condition

---

CALIFORNIA: Similar to Federal provision

CONNECTICUT: Similar to Federal provision, additionally to provide care to spouse's parent or to serve as an organ or bone marrow donor

---

DISTRICT OF COLUMBIA: Similar to Federal provisions, but applied in terms of "family membership," defined to include a person to whom the employee is related by blood, legal custody, or marriage, sharing mutual residence and committed relationship with the Employee. Also includes a child who lives with an employee and for whom the employee permanently assumes and discharges parental responsibility.

HAWAII: Similar to Federal provision (except statute does not apply to employee's own health condition or foster care); it additionally includes leave to care for an employee's parent-in-law and grandparent or grandparent-in-law and an employee's reciprocal beneficiary.

MAINE: Similar to Federal provisions, except adoption leave only if child 16 or younger; no foster care provision

MINNESOTA: For birth or adoption and school and personal sick leave to attend to a child

NEW JERSEY: Birth, adoption placement, serious health condition of child, parent, parent-in-law, or spouse, but not for an employee's own health condition.

OREGON: "Family leave" to care for an infant or newly adopted child under 18 years of age, or for an adopted or foster child older than 18 years of age if the child is incapable of self-care, a family member with a serious health condition because of a mental or physical disability, to recover from the Employee's own serious health condition, to care for the Employee's child who is suffering from an illness, injury, or condition that is not a serious health condition, but requires home care; A female Employee may take a total of 12 weeks of additional leave within any one-year period for an illness, injury or condition related to pregnancy or childbirth that disables the Employee from performing any available job duties; An Employee who takes 12 weeks of "parental leave" (see above) may take an additional 12 weeks to care for a child of the Employee who is suffering from an illness, injury or condition that is not a serious health condition but that requires home care; Two family members of the same Employer may not take concurrent family leave except under limited circumstances; Teachers have special rules

RHODE ISLAND: Similar to federal provision, but includes care for parents-in-law

VERMONT: Similar to Federal provision, additionally including care for parents-in-law

WASHINGTON: Birth, adoption of a child under age 6, or to provide care for a child under 18 with a terminal health condition

WISCONSIN: Birth, adoption, serious health condition of employee, parent, parent-in-law, child or spouse

## *PROVISION: SERIOUS HEALTH CONDITION*

**FEDERAL:** Illness, injury, impairment, or physical or mental condition involving incapacity or treatment connected with inpatient care in hospital, hospice, or residential medical-care facility; or, continuing treatment by a health care provider involving a period of incapacity: (1) requiring absence of more than 3 consecutive calendar days from work, school, or other activities; (2) due to a chronic or long-term condition for which treatment may be ineffective; (3) absences to receive multiple treatments (including recovery periods) for a condition that if left untreated likely would result in incapacity of more than 3 days; or (4) due to any incapacity related to pregnancy or for prenatal care

**CALIFORNIA:** Similar to Federal provision

**CONNECTICUT:** Similar to Federal provision

**DISTRICT OF COLUMBIA:** Similar to Federal provisions

**HAWAII:** Similar to Federal provision

**MAINE:** Similar to Federal provisions, but without specificity regarding length of incapacity

**MINNESOTA:** Except for limited purpose discussed above, no leave for health condition of self or others

**NEW JERSEY:** Similar to Federal provision

**OREGON:** Illness, injury, impairment, or physical or mental condition that requires inpatient care in a hospital, hospice, or residential medical care facility; Illness, disease, or condition that in the medical judgment of the treating health care provider poses an imminent danger of death, is terminal in prognosis with a reasonable possibility of death in the near future, or requires constant care; or any period of disability due to pregnancy, or period of absence for prenatal care

**RHODE ISLAND:** Similar to Federal provision, but no specific provision regarding prenatal care

**VERMONT:** An accident, serious illness, disease, or mental condition that 1) poses imminent danger of death, 2) requires inpatient care in a hospital, or 3) requires continuing in-home care under the direction of a physician

**WASHINGTON:** Care of a child with a terminal health condition

**WISCONSIN:** A disabling physical or mental illness, injury, impairment or condition involving inpatient care in a hospital, nursing home or hospice; or outpatient care that requires continuing treatment or supervision by a health care provider

## *PROVISION: HEALTH CARE PROVIDER*

FEDERAL: Doctors of medicine or osteopathy authorized to practice medicine or surgery; podiatrists, dentists, clinical psychologists, clinical social workers, optometrists, chiropractors (limited to manual manipulation of spine to correct subluxation shown to exist by x-ray), nurse practitioners, and nurse-midwives, if authorized to practice under State law and consistent with the scope of their authorization; Christian Science practitioners listed with the First Church of Christ, Scientist in Boston, MA; any provider so recognized by the Employer or its group health plan's benefits manager; and any health provider listed above who practices and is authorized to practice in a country other than the United States

CALIFORNIA: Medical physician, surgeon, or osteopathic physician certified by California or licensed in another jurisdiction

CONNECTICUT: Similar to Federal provision

DISTRICT OF COLUMBIA: Any person licensed under Federal, State, or District of Columbia law to provide health care services

HAWAII: Person qualified by the Director of Labor and Industrial Relations to render health care and service and who has a license to the practice of medicine, dentistry, chiropractic, osteopathy, naturopathy, optometry, podiatry

MAINE: Doctor of medicine or osteopathy who is licensed in State or any other person determined by the Secretary of Labor to be capable of providing health care services; see below regarding certification by practitioner of spiritual healing arts

MINNESOTA: No provision for leave for serious health condition

NEW JERSEY: No specific provision

OREGON: Similar to federal provision, but does not include language extending recognition to any provider recognized as such by the Employer or its group health plan's benefits manager, includes naturopaths and direct entry midwives.

RHODE ISLAND: No specific definition

VERMONT: No specific provision

WASHINGTON: Licensed physician, osteopathic physician, or surgeon

WISCONSIN: Similar to Federal provision, but also including licensed or certified physician, physician assistant, respiratory care practitioner, physical therapist, dietician, athletic trainer, occupational therapist, pharmacist, acupuncturist, social worker.

## *PROVISION: INTERMITTENT LEAVE*

FEDERAL: Permitted for serious health condition when medically necessary. Not permitted for care of newborn or new placement by adoption or foster care unless Employer agrees

CALIFORNIA: Leave may be taken in one or more periods not to exceed 12 weeks

CONNECTICUT: Similar to Federal provision

DISTRICT OF COLUMBIA: Intermittent leave may be taken when a family member or the Employee himself or herself has a serious health condition

HAWAII: Permitted for birth, adoption placement, and serious health condition of family member

MAINE: No specific provisions

MINNESOTA: No specific provision

NEW JERSEY: Similar to Federal provision

OREGON: Similar to Federal provision

RHODE ISLAND: No specific provision

VERMONT: No specific provision, but short-term family leave (discussed above) requires Employees to make reasonable attempt to schedule appointments outside regular work hours and to provide earliest possible notice

WASHINGTON: Reduced leave schedule is allowed

WISCONSIN: Employee may schedule medical leave as medically necessary and partial absences for family leave in a manner that does not unduly disrupt the Employer's operations

## *PROVISION: SUBSTITUTION OF PAID LEAVE*

FEDERAL: Employees may elect or Employers may require accrued paid leave to be substituted in some cases. No limits on substituting paid vacation or personal leave. An Employee may not substitute paid sick, medical, or family leave for any situation not covered by any Employers' leave plan

CALIFORNIA: For family care and medical leave, Employee may elect, or Employer may require, substitution of accrued vacation leave or other accrued time off or other paid or unpaid time off negotiated with the Employer; For Employee's own serious health condition (but not other purposes unless the Employer and Employee agree), Employee may use accrued sick leave

CONNECTICUT: Similar to Federal provision

DISTRICT OF COLUMBIA: Employee may elect accrued paid family, vacation, personal, or compensatory leave to be substituted, plus the Employee may utilize program run by Employer to use paid leave of another Employee under certain conditions that have been met

HAWAII: Employer or Employee may elect to substitute Employee accrued paid leave provided sick leave may not be substituted unless such leave is normally granted for such family leave purposes, or upon mutual agreement by Employer and Employee

MAINE: If the Employer provides paid family medical leave for fewer than 10 weeks, the additional weeks of leave added to attain the total of 10 weeks may be unpaid

MINNESOTA: Employee may use paid sick leave provided by Employer

NEW JERSEY: Family leave required by this Act may be paid, unpaid, or a combination of paid and unpaid leave; If an employer provides paid family leave for fewer than 12 weeks, the additional weeks of leave added to attain the 12-workweek total required by this Act may be unpaid.

OREGON: Employee may use any paid accrued vacation or sick leave offered by Employer

RHODE ISLAND: Paid leave may be substituted

VERMONT: Employee has option of using accrued sick, vacation, or other paid leave, not to exceed 6 weeks

WASHINGTON: Employer may permit substitution of accrued paid leave

WISCONSIN: Employee may elect to substitute accrued paid or unpaid leave

## *PROVISION: REINSTATEMENT RIGHTS*

FEDERAL: Must be restored to same position or one equivalent to it in all benefits and other terms and conditions of employment

CALIFORNIA: Similar to Federal provision

CONNECTICUT: Unlike Federal (which does not require restoration if the Employee is unable to perform an essential function of his job), if upon return from leave, the Employee is medically unable to perform the Employee's original job, the Employee is to be transferred to work suitable to such Employee's physical condition if such work is available

DISTRICT OF COLUMBIA: Similar to Federal provision, with the addition that if the Employee accepted alternative employment with Employer throughout the duration of the serious health condition, the Employee shall be returned to his or her original employment upon their return from leave

HAWAII: Similar to Federal provision

MAINE: Similar to Federal provision

MINNESOTA: For birth or adoption leave, employee is entitled to return to former position or in a position of comparable duties, hours, and pay. Employee returning from an absence of longer than one month must notify Employer at least 2 weeks prior to return from leave; For school and personal sick leave to attend to a child, employees entitled to return to former position

NEW JERSEY: Similar to Federal provision

OREGON: Employee must be restored to same position – if it still exists; if not, Employee must be restored to any available equivalent position with all terms and conditions at a job located within 20 miles of the site of the employee's former position.

RHODE ISLAND: Similar to Federal provision

VERMONT: Similar to Federal provision

WASHINGTON: Right to be returned to an equivalent position in a workplace within 20 miles of the Employee's previous workplace

WISCONSIN: Similar to Federal provision

## PROVISION: KEY EMPLOYEE EXCEPTION

FEDERAL: Limited exception for salaried Employees if among highest paid 10%, within 75 miles of worksites, restoration would lead to grievous economic harm to Employer, and other conditions met

CALIFORNIA: Similar to Federal provision

CONNECTICUT: No provision

DISTRICT OF COLUMBIA: Similar to Federal provision but for Employers with less than 50 Employees, Employment restoration may be denied to a salaried Employee if the Employee is among the 5 highest paid Employees of an Employer

HAWAII: No similar provision

MAINE: No specific provision

MINNESOTA: No specific provision

NEW JERSEY: Similar to Federal provision, except limited to Employees who are among the highest paid 5% or the seven highest paid Employees, whichever is greater

OREGON: No provision

RHODE ISLAND: Similar to Federal provision

VERMONT: Employer not required to offer Employee return to work if Employee performed unique services and hiring a permanent replacement during the leave after giving reasonable notice to the Employee of intent to do so was only alternative available to Employer to prevent substantial and grievous economic injury

WASHINGTON: Allows Employer to exempt highest paid 10% of Employees or up to 10% of workforce designated as key personnel

WISCONSIN: No specific provision

## PROVISION: MAINTENANCE OF HEALTH BENEFITS DURING LEAVE

FEDERAL: Health insurance must be continued under same conditions as prior to leave

CALIFORNIA: Similar to Federal provision

CONNECTICUT: No specific provision

DISTRICT OF COLUMBIA: Similar to Federal provision

HAWAII: No specific provision

MAINE: No specific provision

MINNESOTA: For birth or adoption leave, employer must make coverage available under any group insurance policy, group subscriber contract or health care plan for Employee and dependents. Employer not required to pay insurance costs

NEW JERSEY: Similar to Federal provision

OREGON: No requirement for continuation of benefits unless required by agreement or policy

RHODE ISLAND: Health benefits must be maintained for duration of leave; Employee to pay total cost of premium prior to commencement of leave with payment to be returned by Employer within 10 days of return to work

VERMONT: Employer is to continue all employment benefits; Employee may be required to pay entire cost of benefits during the leave at existing Employee rate of contribution.

WASHINGTON: If Employer contributions to medical or dental benefits are not required by Employer policy or collective bargaining agreement, Employee may continue coverage at own expense. Employee's expense cannot exceed 102% of the applicable premium

WISCONSIN: Similar to Federal provision

## *PROVISION: LEAVE REQUESTS*

FEDERAL: To be made by Employee at least 30 days prior to date leave is to begin where need is known in advance or, where not foreseeable, as soon as practicable; If due to a planned medical treatment or for intermittent leave, the Employee, subject to health care provider's approval, shall make a reasonable effort to schedule it in a way that does not unduly disrupt Employer's operation

CALIFORNIA: If need for leave is foreseeable, Employee shall provide reasonable advance notice; Similar to Federal provision

CONNECTICUT: Similar to Federal provision

DISTRICT OF COLUMBIA: Similar to Federal provision in that the Employee shall provide reasonable prior notice; Similar to Federal provision

HAWAII: If foreseeable, to be made by Employee in a manner that is practical and reasonable; No similar provision relating to scheduling of medical treatment

MAINE: Made by Employee 30 days in advance unless prevented by medical emergency

MINNESOTA: For birth or adoption leave, employer may adopt reasonable policies governing the timing of requests for unpaid leave

NEW JERSEY: Employee shall provide the employer notice of the expected leave in a manner that is reasonable and practicable

OREGON: Similar to Federal provision, but where 30 day notice not possible, oral request must be made within 24 hours of leave commencement followed by written notice within 3 days after return to work

RHODE ISLAND: Employee shall give at least 30 days notice unless prevented by medical emergency; No provision relating to scheduling

VERMONT: Made by Employee with reasonable notice; For adoption placement or birth, Employer may not require more than 6 weeks advance notice

WASHINGTON: 30 days in advance for birth or adoption unless birth is premature, placement is unanticipated or mother is incapacitated to a point where she cannot care for the child. With these conditions, notice should be as soon as possible but at least within 1 working day of the event. 14 days is required for foreseeable family leave or within 1 working day where it is not foreseeable

WISCONSIN: Made by an Employee in advance in a reasonable and practicable manner; similar to Federal provision insofar as an Employee is required to make a reasonable effort to schedule medical treatment

### PROVISION: MEDICAL CERTIFICATION MAY BE REQUIRED FOR THE FOLLOWING:

FEDERAL: Request for leave because of serious health condition; To demonstrate Employee's fitness to return to work from medical leave where Employer has a uniformly applied practice or policy to require such certification

CALIFORNIA: Request for leave because of serious health condition; Employee's fitness to return to work from medical leave as long as practice of requesting a certificate is uniformly applied

CONNECTICUT: Similar to Federal provision

DISTRICT OF COLUMBIA: Similar to Federal provision; No provision relating to certification of fitness to return to work

HAWAII: Request for leave because of serious health condition; other means of certification for birth or adoption placement; No similar provision

MAINE: From physician to verify amount of leave requested by Employee; may be provided by accredited practitioner relying on prayer or spiritual means; No provision regarding fitness to return to work

MINNESOTA: No specific provision; No provision relating to certification of fitness to return to work

NEW JERSEY: Request may be made for circumstances of birth, adoption placement or because of serious health condition of family member; No provision relating to certification of fitness to return to work.

OREGON: Employer may require certification for family leave taken in relation to a family member with a serious health condition, the employee's own serious health condition, or a child suffering from an illness, injury, or condition that is not a serious health condition but requires home care; Employer may require certification that the Employee is able to resume work

RHODE ISLAND: For leave where Employee is under physician's care; No provision relating to certification for return of Employee to work

VERMONT: Employer may request certification from a physician for serious illness; No specific provision relating to Employee certification for return to work

WASHINGTON: Employer may request certification because of child's birth or terminal illness; No provision relating to certification of fitness to return to work

WISCONSIN: Employer may request certification for serious health condition; No provision relating to certification of fitness to return to work

***PROVISION: ELIGIBILITY OF EXECUTIVE, ADMINISTRATIVE AND PROFESSIONAL EMPLOYEES***

FEDERAL: Such individuals are entitled to FMLA benefits. However, their use of FMLA leave does not change their status under the Fair Labor Standards Act (FLSA), i.e., an Employer does not lose its exemption from the FLSA's minimum wage and overtime requirements.

CALIFORNIA: No specific provision

CONNECTICUT: No specific provision

DISTRICT OF COLUMBIA: No provision regarding effect on exempt status under the District of Columbia minimum wage and overtime law

HAWAII: No similar provision

MAINE: No specific provision

MINNESOTA: No specific provision

NEW JERSEY: No specific provision

OREGON: Similar to Federal provision when FMLA applies, but not in cases when only OFLA applies.

RHODE ISLAND: No specific provision

VERMONT: No specific provision

WASHINGTON: No similar provision

WISCONSIN: No specific provision

# GLOSSARY

**ADA**—The Americans With Disabilities Act (42 USC 12101 et seq.).

**Administrator**—The Administrator of the Wage and Hour Division, Employment Standards Administration, U.S. Department of Labor, including any official of the Wage and Hour Division authorized to perform any of the functions of the Administrator under the FMLA.

**COBRA**—The continuation coverage requirements of Title X of the Consolidated Omnibus Budget Reconciliation Act of 1986.

**Continuing Treatment**—A serious health condition involving continuing treatment by a health care provider.

**Eligible Employee**—An employee who meets the requirements set forth in the FMLA.

**Employ**—To permit to work.

**Employee**—Any individual employed by an employer.

**Employee Employed in an Instructional Capacity**—Teacher.

**Employer**—For purposes of the FMLA, refers to any person engaged in commerce or in an industry or activity affecting commerce who employs 50 or more employees for each working day during each of 20 or more calendar work weeks in the current or preceding calendar year.

**Employment Benefits**—All benefits provided or made available to employees by an employer, including group life insurance, health insurance, disability insurance, sick leave, annual leave, educational benefits, and pensions, regardless of whether such benefits are provided by a practice or written policy of an employer or through an employee benefit plan.

**FLSA**—The Fair Labor Standards Act (29 U.S.C. 201 et seq.).

**FMLA**—The Family and Medical Leave Act of 1993, Public Law 103-3 (February 5, 1993), 107 Stat. 6 (29 U.S.C. 2601 et seq.).

**Foster care**—Foster care is 24-hour care for children in substitution for, and away from, their parents or guardian. Such placement is made by or with the agreement of the State as a result of a voluntary agreement between the parent or guardian that the child be removed from the home, or pursuant to a judicial determination of the necessity for foster care, and involves agreement between the State and foster family that the foster family will take care of the child. Although foster care may be with relatives of the child, State action is involved in the removal of the child from parental custody for the FMLA to apply.

**Group Health Plan**—Any plan of, or contributed to by, an employer, including a self-insured plan, to provide health care, directly or otherwise, to the employer's employees, former employees, or the families of such employees or former employees.

**Health Care Provider**—For purposes of the FMLA, refers to a doctor of medicine or osteopathy who is authorized to practice medicine or surgery by the State in which the doctor practices; podiatrists, dentists, clinical psychologists, optometrists, chiropractors, nurse practitioners, nurse-midwives and clinical social workers authorized to practice under State law and who are performing within the scope of their practice as defined under State law; any health care provider from whom an employer or a group health plan's benefits manager will accept certification of the existence of a serious health condition to substantiate a claim for benefits; and a health care provider as defined above who practices in a country, other than the United States, who is licensed to practice in accordance with the laws and regulations of that country.

**Incapable of Self-Care**—For purposes of the FMLA, refers to an individual who requires active assistance or supervision to provide daily self-care in several of the activities of daily living, such as caring appropriately for one's grooming and hygiene, bathing, dressing and eating, cooking, cleaning, shopping, taking public transportation, paying bills, maintaining a residence, using telephones and directories, using a post office, etc.

**Instructional Employee**—Teacher.

**Intermittent Leave**—Leave taken in separate periods of time due to a single illness or injury, rather than for one continuous period of time, and may include leave of periods from an hour or more to several weeks.

**Parent**—The biological parent of an employee or an individual who stands or stood in loco parentis to an employee when the employee was a child.

**Person**—For purposes of the FMLA, refers to an individual, partnership, association, corporation, business trust, legal representative, or any organized group of persons, including a public agency.

**Physical or Mental Disability**—A physical or mental impairment that substantially limits one or more of the major life activities of an individual.

**Public Agency**—The government of the United States; the government of a State or political subdivision thereof; any agency of the United States, a State, or a political subdivision of a State, or any interstate governmental agency.

**Reduced Leave Schedule**—A leave schedule that reduces the usual number of hours per workweek, or hours per workday, of an employee.

**Secretary**—the Secretary of Labor or authorized representative.

**Son or Daughter**—A biological, adopted, or foster child, a stepchild, a legal ward, or a child of a person standing in loco parentis, who is under 18 years of age or 18 years of age or older and incapable of self-care because of a mental or physical disability.

**Spouse**—A husband or wife as defined or recognized under State law for purposes of marriage in the State where the employee resides, including common law marriage in States where it is recognized.

**State**—Any State of the United States or the District of Columbia or any Territory or possession of the United States.

**Teacher**—An employee employed principally in an instructional capacity by an educational agency or school whose principal function is to teach and instruct students in a class, a small group, or an individual setting, and includes athletic coaches, driving instructors, and special education assistants such as signers for the hearing impaired.

# BIBLIOGRAPHY AND ADDITIONAL RESOURCES

*Black's Law Dictionary, Fifth Edition.* St. Paul, MN: West Publishing Company, 1979.

The Equal Employment Opportunity Commission (Date Visited: August 2005) <http://www.eeoc.gov/>.

The United States Department of Labor (Date Visited: August 2005) <http://www.dol.gov/>.

The Department of Labor, Veterans' Employment and Training (VETS) (Date Visited: August 2005) <http://www.dol.gov/vets/>.